CULTURE SMART!
JAMAICA

Nick Davis

·K·U·P·E·R·A·R·D·

ISBN 978 1 85733 528 6
This book is also available as an e-book: eISBN 978 1 85733 565 1

British Library Cataloguing in Publication Data
A CIP catalogue entry for this book is available from the British Library

First published in Great Britain
by Kuperard, an imprint of Bravo Ltd
59 Hutton Grove, London N12 8DS
Tel: +44 (0) 20 8446 2440 Fax: +44 (0) 20 8446 2441
www.culturesmart.co.uk
Inquiries: sales@kuperard.co.uk

Series Editor Geoffrey Chesler
Design Bobby Birchall

Printed in Malaysia

About the Author

NICK DAVIS is the BBC's Jamaica Correspondent, reporting for TV, Online, and Radio from the Caribbean. A graduate of Leeds Trinity University College and the University College of Falmouth, Nick specializes in Caribbean affairs and the West Indian diaspora in Britain. His parents went to the United Kingdom from Jamaica in the 1960s and returned to the island when he was sixteen. He has lived between the two countries ever since, helping to run their guesthouse on the North Coast. He also contributes regularly as a broadcaster on public radio in the USA and for CBC in Canada.

The Culture Smart! series is continuing to expand.
For further information and latest titles visit
www.culturesmart.co.uk

The publishers would like to thank **CultureSmart!**Consulting for its help in researching and developing the concept for this series.

CultureSmart!Consulting creates tailor-made seminars and consultancy programs to meet a wide range of corporate, public-sector, and individual needs. Whether delivering courses on multicultural team building in the USA, preparing Chinese engineers for a posting in Europe, training call-center staff in India, or raising the awareness of police forces to the needs of diverse ethnic communities, it provides essential, practical, and powerful skills worldwide to an increasingly international workforce.

For details, visit www.culturesmartconsulting.com

CultureSmart!Consulting and **CultureSmart!** guides have both contributed to and featured regularly in the weekly travel program "Fast Track" on BBC World TV.

contents

Map of Jamaica	7
Introduction	8
Key Facts	10
Chapter 1: LAND AND PEOPLE	**12**
• Geographical Snapshot	12
• Climate	14
• Population	15
• A Brief History	16
• Government and Politics	26
• The Economy	30
Chapter 2: VALUES AND ATTITUDES	**32**
• Pride	32
• Religion	32
• Family	34
• Attitudes Toward Others	35
• Sexual Encounters	36
• Attitudes Toward Women	37
• Children	38
• Foreigners	38
• Other Islanders	39
• Work	41
• Education	43
• A Sense of Style	44
• Home Ownership	45
• Cool Jamaica	46
• Political Attitudes	46
• Attitude Toward the Queen	47
• Migration	48
• Attitudes Toward Money	49
• Attitudes Toward Color	50
• Macho Culture	50
Chapter 3: CUSTOMS AND TRADITIONS	**52**
• Christianity	52
• African Religions	54
• Rastafari	56

- National Holidays   61
- Jamaican Traditions   63
- Carnival   65
- Good and Bad Luck Omens   66

Chapter 4: MAKING FRIENDS   **68**
- Who's Genuine?   69
- Meeting People   70
- Greetings   71
- Timekeeping   72
- Gift Giving   72
- Begging   74
- Photography   75
- Invitations Home   75
- Socializing With the Opposite Sex   76

Chapter 5: FAMILY LIFE   **78**
- Family Occasions   79
- Daily Life   81
- Growing Up in Jamaica   84
- Health Services   89
- Housing   90

Chapter 6: TIME OUT   **92**
- Eating Out and Eating In   92
- Drinking   95
- The Beach   97
- What to Wear   98
- Giving "a Small Change"   100
- Town Squares and Shopping Malls   100
- Sports and Exercise   101
- Cultural Life   104
- Nightlife   108
- Places to Visit   114

Chapter 7: TRAVEL, HEALTH, AND SAFETY   **122**
- Route Taxis   123
- "Coasters"   124

contents

- Driving   126
- Pedal Power   130
- Trains   130
- Planes   130
- Where to Stay   131
- Health   132
- Safety   136

Chapter 8: BUSINESS BRIEFING   **138**
- The Economic Climate   138
- Jamaican Business   140
- The Work Force   141
- Government and Business   142
- The Business Relationship   144
- Corruption   145
- Business Gifts   146
- Meetings   146
- Negotiations   148
- Managing Disagreement   149
- Women in Business   149

Chapter 9: COMMUNICATING   **150**
- Language   150
- Forms of Address   151
- Greetings   152
- Directness and Expletives   152
- Humor   153
- Body Language   154
- The Media   156
- Services   158
- Conclusion   160

Appendix: Some Jamaican English Terms   **162**
Further Reading   **165**
Index   **166**

Map of Jamaica

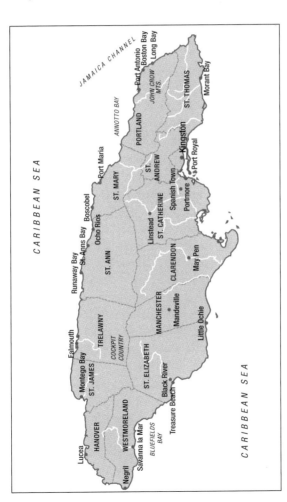

introduction

Jamaica has world recognition. There may be millions of people who cannot pinpoint it on a map but who will have heard of it, helped in no small part by the contribution of its bass-heavy heritage—it's one of the only countries with its own soundtrack. Jamaica is known internationally through Bob Marley, the king of reggae, and from the slow, old-school ska through to reggae and dancehall, its musical legacy looms large. This island overachieves for its small size, and its people are bursting with energy and drive— Jamaica's dominance in athletics is just another example of that.

Jamaica is a country of contradictions. Its image as a sun-drenched tropical paradise with a laid-back attitude conflicts sharply with its reputation for violence, particularly in the capital, Kingston. The country suffers from a PR problem, much of which has been created by tabloid headlines written thousands of miles away, painting a picture that bears no relation to the lives of most people on the island.

Music and sports aside, Jamaica's greatest export and asset is its warm, strong, and spirited people. Their ancestors, forced into a system designed to break the human spirit, remained unbroken. Despite the many hurdles the country still has to clear, the overriding feeling is that the Jamaicans will do it.

The largest of the English-speaking Caribbean countries, Jamaica was one of the jewels in the Imperial British Crown. Many of the ruling class in the smaller islands of the Caribbean educated their sons and daughters there, and it was the administrative center for the region. It is still of vital importance to the United Kingdom.

The country's recent history has been dominated by the rocky road to independence and the path its leaders have since trodden. It went from a situation where a small minority controlled much of the wealth to a form of socialism that saw much of that same wealth and experience flee. Politics looked ready to consume the country in the early 1980s, when it was on the verge of civil war and nightly curfews were the norm, as it became another front in the Cold War.

There is a great deal more to Jamaica, however, than its troubled politics or the palm-fringed beaches and "all-inclusive" holiday resorts that have come to typify it. One of the most intriguing countries in the region, it leaves an impression that is, like the character of its people, larger than life. *Culture Smart! Jamaica* will take you through the gates and beyond the clichés to the real life of the island. It will show you the roots and explain the nuances of modern-day Jamaican society, and help you to enjoy and make the most of your visit to this amazing and invigorating country.

Key Facts

Official Name	Jamaica	A member of CARICOM, OAS, and the Commonwealth
Capital City	Kingston	Kingston had a pop. of 96,052 in the last census in 2001. Including the parish of St Andrew there were 667,778 in 2009.
Main Cities	Spanish Town, Portmore, May Pen, Mandeville, Ocho Rios, Port Antonio, Negril, Montego Bay	
Area	4,244 sq. miles (10,991 sq. km)	
Climate	Tropical. Hurricanes frequent from July to November	
Population	2.7 million (2009 est.)	
Ethnic Makeup	Black 91.2%, mixed 6.2%, other or unknown 2.6% (2001 census)	
Languages	English, English Patois	
Religion	Christianity is the dominant faith (65 percent). Major Protestant denominations include Seventh-day Adventist, Church of God, Baptist, and Pentecostal.	There is a small but significant Roman Catholic community. Rastafari (1 percent); others include Revivalisim and Kumina. Small Hindu, Muslim, and Jewish communities

Government	Bicameral parliament: Senate and House of Representatives	Senate appointed by the governor general on recommendations of the prime minister and the leader of opposition. Ruling party allocated 13 seats, opposition 18. The House of Representatives has 60 seats. MPs elected by popular vote to serve 5-year terms
Currency	Jamaican Dollar (J$)	US dollars are widely accepted in tourist resorts; Canadian dollars and British pounds are easily exchanged
Media	Three national TV stations: TVJ, CVM, and Love TV. 23 national radio stations	Newspapers include *The Gleaner*, *The Observer*, *The Star*, *Chat*, *X News*, and *The Sunday Herald*
Electricity	110 volts, at 50 cycles. Some hotels also have 220-volt supply	
Video/TV	TV and videos use the NTSC system	
Internet Domain	.jm	
Telephone	Country code is 876	
Time Zone	Standard Time is 5 hours behind GMT	

chapter one

LAND &
PEOPLE

GEOGRAPHICAL SNAPSHOT

The third-largest island in the Caribbean, Jamaica lies some 90 miles (144 km) south of Cuba. It has an area of 4,243 square miles (10,991 sq. km), with mountains, beaches, coastal plains, and rain forests in many parts of the island, sometimes within less than an hour's drive of each other. The country is long and thin, being only 146 miles (235 km) long and just 51 miles (82 km) wide at its widest point.

Jamaica, known as the Rock, is a much more hilly and mountainous country than the neighboring Cuba and Hispaniola. The land rises steeply up to 7,500 feet (2,300 m) at its highest in the Blue Mountains. The mountains run like a spine through the southeast of the island, and can be seen from both north and south coasts.

The country is rich in limestone, with large deposits of the mineral over much of the island's surface. In central areas, such as the Cockpit Country in Trelawney, the soft stone has been eaten away by river water that has created a landscape of sinkholes and hillocks resembling upside-down egg cartons. The springwater of Jamaica in the past was considered to be of extremely high quality because of the limestone working as a filter down to the watershed. However, the mining of one of Jamaica's other resources, bauxite, has been blamed for poisoning some of the water supplies. The waste from the process of turning bauxite into alumina results in a toxic red mud. In the past this was disposed of by pumping the waste into old mine workings; this created red mud lakes that leached the dangerous chemical by-products into the groundwater table, and the pollutants seeped into underground reserves, making the water dangerous for human consumption.

In the past there were mangrove forests along much of the island's coastline. However, the swamps and lagoons, seen as wasteland, have been filled in and the trees cut down. Mangroves are essential, their root structure preventing coastal erosion, providing protection from storm surge during hurricanes, and making a protective habitat for young fish and sea creatures.

Some of Jamaica's landmass is protected in national and local reserves, such as three national parks—the Blue and John Crow Mountains, which have some of the greatest biodiversity in the Caribbean, the Montego Bay Marine Park, and

the Negril Marine Park. Other protected sites
are forest reserves, which include the Cockpit
Country, Portland Bight, Black River in St.
Elizabeth, and Lovers Leap.

CLIMATE

Jamaica has a tropical marine climate with
temperatures averaging between around 66°F
(19°C) and 87°F (31°C). The trade winds and sea
breezes generally provide respite from the hot
summer temperatures, but in the cities, especially
Kingston and May Pen, the daytime heat borders
on the unbearable.

May and October are the wettest months in
Jamaica. The average annual rainfall is in the
region of 50.7 inches (128 cm), but the variations
around the country are great. The northern slopes
of the Blue Mountains may have 200 inches
(508 cm) of rain a year, while the drier, sheltered
south coast may see about 30 inches (76 cm). The
downpours are often torrential, but the sun comes
back in a short time and "burns away" the water,
as locals say, in a few hours. In Kingston it's not
uncommon to see parts of the city flooded and in
the space of a few minutes' drive see other areas
that look as if they've been hit by a drought.

Hurricanes

The frequency of the breeze—as Jamaicans like to
call anything above a tropical storm—has
increased in the past decade. Jamaica has faced a

direct threat from hurricanes every year since 2001. The storms accompanying the Atlantic hurricane season, which runs from June 1 to November 30, have become an annual feature of life, and their names have become etched into the national consciousness by the damage they've wreaked. Despite being in the hurricane belt the island seemed to miss out on many of the storms for decades until 1988, when Hurricane Gilbert left forty-five people dead and caused millions of dollars' worth of damage. Hurricane Ivan in 2004 left seventeen dead, and Gustav in 2008 caused the death of fifteen.

Preparedness for hurricanes is efficient. Emergency procedures are printed in all local newspapers and broadcast on radio. Most hotels have the same information posted or available from the front desk. Hotels are built to withstand hurricane force winds, as are most recent buildings on the island.

Jamaica is divided into fourteen administrative parishes. The country also has three counties, but these are purely historical and date back to the start of English rule. Cornwall County covers the west of the island, Middlesex the central regions, and Surrey the eastern areas. The fourteen parishes each have a capital as its administrative center.

POPULATION

According to the last census, in 2001, around 91 percent of Jamaica's population are black of

African descent. Other ethnic groups include East Indian (1.3 percent), Chinese (0.2 percent) and white Jamaicans of British, Irish, and German ancestry (0.2 percent). People of mixed heritage are estimated to make up around 6.2 percent.

There has been a recent increase in the number of migrants from China and Africa. Haitians, Cubans, Colombians, and others from Latin American countries have also settled in the country, along with returnees—Jamaicans who went to work abroad who have "come home" from the USA, Canada, and the UK to retire.

There is a large divide between rich and poor, with a wealthy upper class and a growing middle class, especially in urban centers such as Montego Bay and Mandeville. Jamaica has done much to reduce poverty, but it's been estimated that around 14 percent of the population live below the poverty line in rural areas and in the inner-city communities around the island.

A BRIEF HISTORY

The national motto is "Out of Many, One People"—an apt saying for a country in which the fusion of so many cultures has created the unique Jamaican identity and reputation.

The population today is around 2.8 million, with nearly as many Jamaicans living off the island as on it. Leaving the island in search of better opportunities abroad has been a common theme in this nation's history.

The joyful optimism that followed independence in 1962 was soon tempered by political instability and financial indebtedness, which have continued to shape the island's affairs. Its people, though, have found their own ways to survive cheerfully in the present climate.

Origins and Conquest

The original inhabitants of the island were Amerindian people, the Ciboney, who first settled in the region between 5000 and 4000 BCE. The last Amerindian inhabitants of Jamaica were the Taino, a subgroup of the Arawaks. The Taino were a peaceful hunter-gatherer people who had made their way over from the north coast of the South American mainland. They pushed on through the Caribbean islands over centuries, reaching Jamaica between 650 and 900 CE. They were skilled sailors, fishing from huge dugout canoes as well as hunting game and gathering food. They named the country Xaymaca, meaning "Land of Wood and Water."

The Tainos' exclusive use of the land came to an end when Christopher Columbus "discovered" it in May 1494. He captured the island in the name of the Spanish Crown, named it Santiago, and claimed it for himself,

to be ruled as his personal property, which the terms of his expedition allowed. When he died in 1506 he bequeathed the island to his son, Diego, who appointed one of the original lieutenants on the journey of discovery, Don Juan Esquivel, as governor.

Spanish settlement began on the north coast of the island, but had to be moved to the south after disease ravaged the colonists. Remains of the old Spanish capital, St. Jago de la Vega, still stand in what is now Spanish Town.

As it was found to have no gold, the island became an almost forgotten part of the Spanish Empire. It served mainly as a stop for picking up rations and repairing and cleaning ships on their way to and from the more prosperous parts of the Empire. Poorly defended, it was exposed to the depredations of raiding parties from French, English, and Dutch pirate ships.

The Spanish settlers continued to eke out an existence, however. They had introduced farming to Santiago and brought horses, pigs, and cattle, but needed a workforce. They had tried to enslave the Tainos, but murder, harsh conditions, European diseases, and in some cases suicide had reduced the Tainos' numbers so drastically that it was necessary to find a fresh source of labor. The Spanish looked to Africa, and started importing slaves from the continent in 1517, in a trade that continued for much of the island's history.

Before long, another seafaring colonial power had its eye on the island: England.

The English Occupation

In 1654 Jamaica came into the sights of Oliver Cromwell, Lord Protector of England. At war with Spain, he called his plan "the Western Design." He gave the task of taking Hispaniola, the second-largest island in the Caribbean, to two of his commanders, General Robert Venables and Admiral William Penn, who made a mess of it and fled with a thousand men. Knowing that failure would be unacceptable, they looked across the Caribbean Sea to Jamaica, which had pretty much been left to its own devices and was a soft target. In May 1655 they landed and took the island, its Spanish inhabitants fleeing to Cuba by boat, leaving virtually nothing behind apart from their slaves. Venables and Penn had gained a dominion but none of the booty that Cromwell had expected, so on their return he promptly locked them in the Tower of London. Their arrival did, however, start the new colonization of Jamaica.

By this time the Taino had been driven to the edge of extinction. Some are believed to have survived and lived in the island's interior

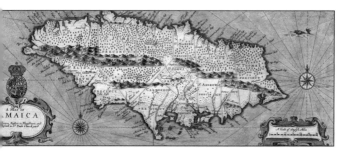

alongside the maroons, the descendants of slaves left by the Spanish, and many of their traditions are still part of Jamaican culture. This was one of the first examples of how Jamaicans learned to blend their diversity of races and creeds to their advantage—it was an early experience of multiculturalism.

Trade soon developed as immigrants from neighboring English colonies, such as Barbados and the Somer islands (Bermuda), as well as from England, settled in Jamaica, encouraged by land grants. However, the fledgling colony was vulnerable to the threat of invasion from the surrounding Spanish islands. Jamaica's governors therefore decided to make a port, Port Royal, available to privateers—state-sanctioned private warships that were authorized to attack foreign powers in return for a share of the profits arising from any vessel they captured. Alongside the pirates they continued to harass the Spanish on the high seas, and by using Jamaica as a base ensured its protection.

Soon Port Royal, which had become one of the wealthiest places on earth, became known as its wickedest. The privateers had to pay for the privilege, handing over a tribute of 10 percent of their share of the booty to the authorities. This continued up until 1692, when a massive earthquake saw most of Port Royal disappear into the sea.

The Plantation Economy

"King sugar," as it became known, dominated the economy, and for centuries the crop thrived in Jamaica's tropical climate. Many of the men who had been part of the initial English invasion were given land rights as a reward, and started planting sugar. By the eighteenth century the island was the largest sugar producer in the world.

The history of Jamaica is bound up with that of sugar. The crop was grown initially in Barbados in the seventeenth century and the trade developed rapidly there, but over time Barbados was unable to compete with the much bigger island of Jamaica and the colony became the natural home of this increasingly valuable commodity.

The need for mass labor in the cane fields led directly to the growth of the transatlantic slave trade. This was one side of a triangular trade— the side known as the "Middle Passage." Manufactured goods from England were shipped to West Africa and exchanged for slaves, who were then transported and sold as labor in the Caribbean, where sugar, rum, and molasses were loaded on to the ships headed back to English ports, such as Liverpool, London, and Bristol, which grew wealthy from the trade.

Over time, the small plantations were unable to compete with the much bigger plantations owned by absentee landlords who lived in the height of luxury in England, made wealthy by high import duties on, and higher taxation of, sugar from other parts of the world. Their slaves lived in inhuman conditions that saw six slaves die for every one born, and the slave ships that carried them to the New World saw an onboard

death rate of about 13 percent. It is estimated that between twelve and fifteen million slaves were transported between 1500 and 1900.

The Maroon Wars

From the late seventeenth century through the eighteenth, the descendants of the slaves released by the Spanish after the English invasion, along with successive runaways, lived as free men and women in the island's mountainous interior. They were known as "maroons"—an anglicized form of the Spanish word *cimarron*, or runaway. They fought against the British and took over large areas of the countryside. They were divided into two main tribes—the Leeward and Windward Maroons. Their guerrilla war eventually led to the signing of peace treaties with the colonists. The first treaty, drawn up in 1739, was to see the maroons given 15,000 acres of land. The final treaty left them with a mere 1,500 acres, because a zero was omitted from the figure in the agreement. The deal allowed them to live semiautonomous lives with their own chief plus a British administrator.

They in return would cease the conflict and not allow any more runaway slaves to join their communities. In fact, they would now be rewarded for apprehending any slaves who escaped.

This created antagonism and eventually led to the Second Maroon War of 1795. The violence erupted when two maroons, guilty of stealing two pigs, were punished by being whipped by a black slave overseer—an affront the proud maroons couldn't accept. The war saw the destruction of all but one of the main maroon communities in Jamaica. Accompong, in St. Elizabeth, was the sole survivor because of the decision by its elders not to fight the British.

The Abolition of Slavery
The island's large enslaved African population vastly outnumbered the white inhabitants. It was estimated that there was a ratio of twenty to one at one point, when the majority of plantation owners were living in England while their overseers looked after day-to-day affairs on the island. There was also a sizeable mixed-race group and a free colored community on the island.

The English eventually outlawed the trading and

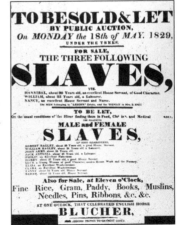

importation of slaves with the Abolition Bill of 1807. However, the practice continued illegally, with a small number of Africans being smuggled on to the island. Eventually, emancipation in 1834, followed by a four-year apprenticeship, saw full freedom for the enslaved Africans in the English-speaking Caribbean in 1838.

The plantation owners were paid millions in compensation for the loss of their free labor and the inconvenience of having to pay wages to their newly liberated workers. Many owners simply sold their land, and, despite their new freedom, conditions barely improved for the former slaves.

Rebellion

In 1866 the economic hardship boiled over, and resulted in the Morant Bay Rebellion in St. Thomas. Led by Paul Bogle, a black church deacon, it saw more than two thousand rebels rioting over the apathy of the island's governor, Edward John Eyre. The uprising was brutally crushed with more than nine hundred people killed, including Bogle himself. Also executed was George William Gordon, a mixed-race politician and businessman from Kingston. He had little to do with the rebellion but was a vocal opponent of the way Jamaica was being run, and the colonial authorities took the opportunity to make an example of him and have him silenced.

Gordon's murder, however, was the catalyst for change in the country. Following the rebellion a Royal Commission was set up to investigate what had happened. Eyre was removed from office and charged twice with the murder of British subjects, but the case never went to court. He left the island in disgrace.

As a result of the Morant Bay Rebellion, the Jamaica Assembly, which had been in place since 1661, decided to renounce its charter. It had consisted of wealthy landowners granted a degree

of self-rule by the Crown with the power to legislate on issues relating to the colony.

Over the centuries a plantation class of island-born whites had developed—the "plantocracy," who wielded political power. The mixed-race children of many of the slave owners also had certain rights not afforded to those of black heritage, whether slave or free. This created a hierarchy that has remained imbedded in Jamaican society. The Creole class straddled the racial divide, having partial access to all segments of society.

Other benefits that came from the Morant Bay inquiry were the introduction of public hospitals and an up-to-date police force. It was also the start of the struggle for the right to vote. At that point "universal" suffrage was allowed only to the privileged white minority.

GOVERNMENT AND POLITICS

Jamaica remained a Crown colony, governed from Whitehall, until August 6, 1962, when it became an independent nation, but the first moves toward self-governance had been established in the late 1930s along with

the formation of the country's first trade union, which ultimately led to the foundation of the two main political parties that still exist today.

The country's political institutions are based on the Westminster bicameral system. An appointed upper house, the Senate, is comprised of twenty-one seats. The prime minister nominates thirteen of the seats, and the leader of the opposition the remaining eight. The House of Representatives is made up of sixty MPs who are elected on a first-past-the-post basis. The parliamentary term is five years.

The head of state is still Queen Elizabeth, but this is more of an honorary role—a remnant of the island's colonial history. Her Majesty's representative on the island is the governor-general, whose role is ceremonial, such as presiding over the swearing-in of judges and other high officials, including members of the cabinet who are appointed on the advice of the prime minister. The Queen and the GG, as most Jamaicans call the governor-general, still technically have the power to dismiss parliament and the prime minister.

Jamaica has traditionally had a two-party system, with power changing over the years between the People's National Party (PNP) and the Jamaica Labour Party (JLP).

Norman Manley founded the PNP in 1938. In 1943, a year before universal adult suffrage became law, Alexander Bustamante, who was Manley's cousin and had been a political ally, formed the JLP. The two men drifted in opposite directions ideologically, with the JLP taking a more liberal capitalist stance as opposed to the democratic socialist leanings of the PNP, where members still describe themselves as comrades.

The JLP were in power from independence in 1962 until a decade later, when the PNP's Michael Manley led the party to victory. His eight years in power were some of the most tumultuous in the nation's history, but he was arguably its most popular leader. His brand of democratic socialism heralded a new era of government spending on social reform, improving the nation's infrastructure and economic independence. Manley also spoke directly to the country's black majority at a time when black power was at its height and color prejudice was still rife on the island. His call that "better must come" was enthusiastically taken up by the disenfranchised, but as he started to nationalize industry his moves were seen by some as a leaning toward communism.

A slowdown in the world economy, a curb on the amount of foreign currency that Jamaicans

were allowed to have, and a rise in violent crime that resulted in a yearlong state of emergency were the final straws for the nation's wealthy and educated white-collar workers. This was the start of the capital flight from Jamaica, the mass migration of the island's professionals who soon found ways to get their money out of the island. Many moved to the USA, Canada, and the UK, often without telling even friends or family. They took with them not only their money but their valuable expertise at a time when the country most needed it. Michael Manley's reaction was to say, "Jamaica has no room for millionaires. For anyone who wants to become a millionaire, we have five flights a day to Miami." This created an enduring feeling in Jamaica that a better life, and better opportunities, can be found abroad, "in foreign," rather than on the island.

The economy continued to slide as the world economy continued to shrink. Manley severed ties with the International Monetary Fund after it insisted that the country take severe austerity measures to qualify for further loans. Many of Manley's supporters were no longer seeing any progress, and in 1980 an election was called. The campaign was the most violent in Jamaica's history, and the country came to the brink of civil war.

Manley lost the election to the JLP's Edward Seaga, but would return to power nine years later. For eighteen years, until September 2007, the PNP was the ruling party under the leadership of Michael Manley, P. J. Patterson, and Portia Simpson-Miller, who became the country's first female prime minister when she took office in 2006.

In the general election of September 3, 2007, the JLP won at the polls with a thirty-three-to-twenty-seven-seat victory, and on September 11, 2007, after being sworn in by Governor-General Kenneth Hall, Bruce Golding assumed office as the ninth prime minister of Jamaica.

THE ECONOMY

Jamaica has a mixed economy—a combination of state and private-sector businesses. Services play a major role, with tourism and mining as the leading sources of foreign exchange. The 1990s saw a return of many industries from state ownership to

the private sector through divestment, but the country has suffered severely with high levels of debt since the 1980s. The IMF put in place austerity measures combined with high interest repayments that were crippling to a nation that had suffered a fall in the gross national product and a slowdown in the global economy, its

bauxite/alumina industry near collapse, and tourism showing a decline—due in part to a rise in crime resulting from the lack of money affecting the country's urban poor.

In the mid to late 1990s the government again borrowed heavily to rescue the economy, and the result of those bailouts caused Jamaica to be saddled with the fourth-highest debt burden per person in the world. The country has constantly fought not to default on its external debts, which now stand at over US$10 billion. Debt servicing, which Jamaica struggles to afford, takes more than half of the country's earnings and leaves very little for the nation to plow back into social programs or to improve the island's infrastructure.

chapter two

VALUES *&* ATTITUDES

PRIDE

Jamaican people have pride in themselves, and a genuine feeling that they can achieve anything. Strangely, there's no other country in the world where the belief in self is more ingrained and yet so strongly concealed. Many people feel that it is Jamaican society itself, as well as the lack of opportunity to advance, that holds them back. Jamaican culture is one of self-expression—but only within the confines of what others deem acceptable, for the country has a vein of conservatism that would surprise many. From the exhibitionism of the dancehall to the strictures of the Church, the opinion of others is the prevailing consideration.

RELIGION

Jamaica is a very Christian country. It has the highest concentration of churches per capita in the world, and the large number of immaculately dressed people to be seen heading for a service on a Saturday or Sunday is a testimony to the devotion Jamaicans have to the Church.

The island also has a baffling number of denominations. The better-known groups include Anglican, Catholic, Baptist, Seventh-day Adventist, and Pentecostal, but there are hundreds of other congregations around the country assembling in an array of houses of the Lord, from purpose-built temples that seat hundreds to simple homes that have been converted and consecrated for worship.

Women vastly outnumber men in the congregations. However, changes in regard to women's taking more leadership in the faith that have taken place in churches elsewhere have not happened in Jamaica. The senior positions, such as pastor, elder, and deacon, are still considered roles that should be filled by men.

Bible study, prayer meetings, and Church conventions mean that virtually every Jamaican knows the Scriptures, and even if they don't attend church regularly they believe in God and Jesus Christ. By heeding the biblical proverb of "Train up a child in the way he should go," and receiving and giving religious instruction from an early age, they grow up with moral guidelines that are passed on through the generations.

FAMILY

Jamaicans have strong family bonds in terms of mutual responsibility. In years gone by, the large extended family would often live together in the home headed by an uncle, aunt, or grandparents.

Having a big yard, a form of compound in which many generations lived together under the same roof, was extremely common until recent years. The Jamaican family is often matriarchal, with large numbers of women having a "baby father," a man who may or may not live with his children. The fact that men and women "give bun"—a term used to describe infidelity—or have multiple partners means that many children grow up with half-brothers and -sisters.

Jamaicans who are abroad in the diaspora will often send back money, clothes, and other goods in barrels to their families at home (see Chapter 4, Gift Giving). The need to make better money abroad has seen parents travel to seek work in the USA, Canada, or the UK, and leave their children at home to be cared for by relatives. There is great concern over these so-called "barrel children," whose only contact with their mothers and fathers for long periods of time is through the presents or money sent for their welfare.

The country is, however, full of contradictions, and the family structure is especially strong within some Christian households where both mother and father are present and the man is often the head of the house. Also, in times gone by older members of the family would be cared for and treated with great respect. However, this is now changing, as some now regard them as a financial drain, and the care of elders is a growing issue in the country.

ATTITUDES TOWARD OTHERS

Jamaicans tend to be emotional and impulse driven. They are a people of extremes. This is borne out by the near-infectious laughter and jokes that are never far away in any social setting. However, when people get angry ("vex") here, the aggression, ferocity, and volume levels make it seem that murder is about to be committed. In most situations hostilities blow over in a short space of time, and the would-be combatants will be friends once again. But being quick to anger can have violent consequences, and is a character trait in Jamaicans that some say is linked to the country's high murder rate.

SEXUAL ENCOUNTERS

The same impetuous attitude may also be the reason for Jamaica's highly sexually charged atmosphere, which is evident in nearly all interaction between men and women. Some of the dance moves on display at Carnival and some of the street dances, such as "Passa Passa," are blatantly sexual. Pretty much everywhere you'll see men and women flirting.

For women, the attention they receive in this macho culture can be quite overwhelming. It often starts with a "psst" sound that men use to attract the attention of a prospective partner. Men will be persistent in trying to secure the phone number of a woman they like, to get a date. However, it's not just the men who are straight to the point. Jamaican women are also very direct in their approach—so much so that a proposition will not leave much to the imagination. Having a partner with you may not always be a deterrent.

Despite the open sexuality of the country, people disapprove of overtly slack behavior and even public displays of affection, such as holding hands and kissing.

ATTITUDES TOWARD WOMEN

Women play second fiddle to men in Jamaica, and are generally not respected as equals in the society. Some of this comes out of a very biblical view of men and women and their roles: the man as provider, the woman as primary caregiver to his child.

The inequality between the sexes in terms of income means that in some cases a woman will actually pick a man and "breed for him"—she will become pregnant so that he will support her financially.

A woman without a child actually carries a social stigma in Jamaica, and people in some communities will question her fertility if she hasn't given birth by the time she has reached her early twenties. Jamaicans often look confused when they meet foreigners who have no children, and you may hear them describe such a person as "a mule," or "barren."

Educationally, a new situation has developed in the island's schools, in that the girls are now outperforming the boys. Greater numbers of young women are going to university, and women are filling more of the key jobs in all sectors of the economy. In the workplace itself, they are respected coworkers. Yet many of the old attitudes remain.

CHILDREN

The Jamaican attitude toward children is that they should behave themselves, and that any misbehavior is a sign that the child is spoiled and needs to "hear or they shall feel." Corporal punishment is considered the only effective way of teaching children the boundaries between good and bad behavior. Most Jamaican children get smacked, and this can range from a mild slap to a severe physical beating with any implement that comes to hand. Most people would class the latter as abuse, but in Jamaican society "sparing the rod" is seen as worse than not raising a child properly.

FOREIGNERS

Generally, Jamaicans are welcoming to foreigners. They are fiercely proud of their country, and as the island is a major tourist destination they are aware how easily negative perceptions can stick. This means that they'll often go out of their way to help. From the slightly annoying guides with mock American accents who will approach you in the street and offer to show you around, to the local in a small rural village, if you show an interest in the country people will interact, smile, and be interested in you, but many do still expect "a little something" in return. Despite emancipation some Jamaicans still show an unusual deference toward white foreigners over visitors of color. Sometimes this higher regard for visiting white people is rooted in jealousy of the fact that nonwhite visitors—people like themselves—have wealth and opportunities that they don't; sometimes it's because visitors from the Jamaican diaspora may not tip as well and may be ruder to them than the white visitors.

Jamaicans are direct and straight to the point when addressing people, so if someone is fat a Jamaican won't be afraid to mention it, and if someone is white they may often call them "Whitey," but it's not intended as an insult—it's just the most obvious way of identifying or differentiating someone, or of getting their attention.

Some men see foreigners—especially the single women, but not exclusively, as they'll try it on with married ones too—as a route to getting off the island. They believe that a sexual spree—and the Jamaican male has a reputation as a lover—is what a lot of visitors want, and also that it might lead to something else. There is an element of "rastitution" and a "rent-a-dred" attitude in Negril, for example, but some men dream of a foreign woman as a passport to the outside world, seeing this as a way to step up in life and better themselves. The reality for many of these "Shirley Valentine" romances is that it's a marriage of convenience, and many women don't realize this until it is too late, having fallen for the sweet nothings of their island lover.

OTHER ISLANDERS
Jamaicans see their own island as far superior to every other in the Caribbean. They are the biggest

English-speaking nation in the region, and have a tradition of calling the residents of the smaller countries in the Anglophone Caribbean "small islanders." For instance, they refer to Barbados as Little England. Most visitors to Barbados from the UK would say that the country is nothing like the British Isles, and Barbadians would probably disagree that their attitudes are similar to that of the mother country. Ask most Jamaicans about Barbados, however, and the attitude remains, despite the fact that many of them have never even visited the island.

There is also a strong political rivalry between Jamaica and Trinidad; back in the late 1950s there was a plan to bring the commonwealth of islands together into a political union, the West Indian Federation. The parliament and headquarters were to be in the Trinidadian capital, Port of Spain, and many Jamaicans were concerned that Jamaica, which was at the time the wealthiest of the nations, would be left to support the smaller, poorer nations, including the twin island republic of Trinidad and Tobago. A referendum was held in Jamaica, the people voted against the Federation, and without Jamaica it quickly collapsed as an institution. The fact that Trinidad is now wealthy because of its large oil deposits and Jamaica is now highly indebted makes a cruel irony indeed.

Many people in the other Caribbean countries see Jamaicans as brash, loud, boastful, and a touch condescending when they describe them as "small islanders." They criticize the island's violent reputation, yet for many of the educated young people from these islands a preferred option is to study in Jamaica at the Mona Campus of the University of the West Indies.

WORK

Jamaica's relaxed pace of life extends in many cases into the workplace. The laid-back attitude that is especially prevalent in the service industries was notoriously bad for years. It has dramatically improved—but don't be surprised if you get a slow response to your quite reasonable requests in restaurants, supermarkets, and stores. "Soon come" is a phrase you may hear—it acknowledges your presence, but does not mean that the speaker will give you his or her attention as soon as you might wish!

"Fast food" as such in Jamaica does not exist. You can wait for what seems an eternity for food you can see lying temptingly over there, ready to be served. A trip to the bank is an all-day affair of waiting in lines that seem to get no shorter, while someone who knows the cashier manages to push in ahead of everyone.

One problem is that some people in Jamaica still conflate service and servitude—a big issue in a former slave society. For them it's demeaning to comply, despite the fact that the customer helps to pay their wages. But the Jamaican contradictions continue, as a strong work ethic also exists within the society; it is generational, and also depends on the work people are doing. Some Jamaican employers do not treat their workers fairly, demanding long hours for low pay because they know that they can replace them easily. Such exploitation leads to employees avoiding going the extra mile, but those same people, if given the opportunity to work abroad for a decent wage, will work themselves to death to provide for their families and a better future.

If you're dealing with government agencies, expect long lines; if you plan to get fast food it won't come quickly, and don't expect the servers to move much faster than a snail's pace. Maybe it's the climate that makes moving with haste such a formidable task, especially in the summer, or it could be that people just don't see the point of rushing. One thing is certain, and that is that people in Jamaica can often identify foreigners by their speed more than anything else.

Initially the slow pace can be annoying, especially if you've got deadlines, or if you're really hungry, and things are moving slowly. Visitors often lose their cool and their tempers over the service, but in most cases this will elicit a laugh as people wonder why you're getting angry about something so trivial. Eventually, you'll just relax into the pace of life.

Sometimes Jamaicans will say what they think you want to hear rather than giving you a straight answer. It's unclear if this is done to get people off their backs or just to be malicious; either way it can make life more difficult. In certain situations, especially if something needs urgent attention, make sure that your instructions are crystal clear and that people know exactly what you expect, because otherwise it may not be done, or not in the way you want. Note that Jamaicans sometimes don't want to ask for help for fear of looking inefficient or stupid and losing face, in which case respect toward them might decline.

The difficulty of getting and keeping good jobs has given rise to a lack of autonomy in the workforce. Bureaucracy can lead to a very long-winded decision-making process, in which even the most basic questions are referred to the boss. It means that management gets bogged down in minutiae and everything slows right down.

EDUCATION

Jamaicans have long had some of the best schools in the Caribbean, and have educated the leaders of the empire around the region, from Bermuda to Barbados—another reason for snobbery toward the smaller islands. Jamaican parents set great store by education, realizing that it can give a child better opportunities.

However, the country has hit a brick wall as a result of a combination of factors. Families have got younger, and girls and boys often have children when they are barely out of school, without having finished their own education. Many people now don't see the importance of it, and don't push their children to learn. The country hasn't been able to finance education as much as it would have liked, and some schools have to operate a shift system because there are too many pupils. The school day is split into two, with some going in the morning and others in the afternoon. Teacher training is at best patchy, resulting in a population with a low functional literacy and an inability to use math and English properly in daily life.

Higher education has been much more meritocratic, with all sections of society represented at university; however, the retention of those students on the island is an ongoing issue. It has been estimated that more than 70 percent of graduates leave the country.

A SENSE OF STYLE

Jamaicans love to turn out looking good. Every laborer will have a change of clothes for heading to or from work; the idea of hitting the street not looking clean and sharp is unthinkable. For the uptown male, it's a button-down shirt tucked into the trousers, and nice shoes; for the corporate woman, a skirt not too short but figure-hugging, with high heels.

When it comes to going out in the evening, that's where the real style is, both up and downtown. The money spent on preparing for a night out would make one wonder if Jamaica is really a middle-income developing nation, when one sees the weaves, nails, hair styling, beard cutting, and haircuts, quite apart from the clothes and the "crepes"—the ubiquitous classic, the Clarke's crepe-soled shoe, is still a fashion statement for young men across the country. The latest designs from the major sneaker manufacturers are on sale not long after they've hit the stores in New York or London. The "higglers," the market traders around the country, seemingly sell what people most need—household products, food, and clothes.

Dancehall music and its racy lyrics are matched with a provocative style of dress. The moves leave little to the imagination, and the outfits worn by the women add to the sexiness that's a key part of the music.

HOME OWNERSHIP

Building one's own home is significant. An Englishman's home may be his castle, but for Jamaicans it actually is. Buying land and building a house is the dream of many, and loose planning regulations mean that some wild designs become reality, often reflecting the personality of the owner. People will often build as big as they can, using nearly every available square foot—a sign of how successful they are. The large houses that you'll find even in modest areas are built out of a belief that the bigger and stronger your home, the better you must be. This is especially true of people who have lived abroad for many years. When they come back to Jamaica, a conspicuous way of showing their success is to build the biggest thing they can out of concrete.

COOL JAMAICA

The island's laid-back attitude, the music, the creativeness, and the straight out-and-out confidence that exudes from virtually every Jamaican is what makes the country cool. Everyone believes that there is a unique, God-given talent within them, which can be their way out of whatever situation they may be in. The modesty that exists in some cultures is lacking in Jamaica, and that has made for a very resilient people. But the trappings of wealth are what many Jamaicans aspire to, so having not only the right clothes but also the right car, house, and even friends is what defines "cool."

POLITICAL ATTITUDES

Jamaica has had democratic elections since its independence in 1962, but the country is riven by political tribalism. There is a divisive split in the nation between supporters of the Jamaica Labour Party and those of the People's National Party. The orange and green of the two groups have come to dominate parts of the country, and it is generally wise not to raise the question of which side of the political divide people sit.

The election of 1980 was particularly violent, with the country struggling to choose between socialism and capitalism as the Cold War made itself felt in the Caribbean. More than seven hundred people were killed as Jamaica came perilously close to civil war. Parts of Kingston became ghettos linked to one or the other party, and were controlled by politicians who used local gangsters, known as "dons," to bolster their support. The dons looked after "their" people, paying for such things as medical expenses and school fees for children, and in return received the unyielding support of the community. Today the dons continue their illegal trade in extortion, prostitution, drugs, and murder, with the support of the bigger men, the politicians, who in the past even helped to secure the votes of an area by getting weapons for the criminal bosses.

ATTITUDE TOWARD THE QUEEN

Jamaicans of a certain generation have always looked favorably toward Britain. The Queen is still the head of state, and Jamaicans born before independence were subjects of the British Empire. They knew more about British history than they knew about their own Caribbean history, and more about European geography than that of the region they lived in. They saw the United Kingdom as the motherland, with many serving and dying for the Crown during both World Wars and in conflicts dating back to the eighteenth century.

GREATER LONDON COUNCIL

MARY SEACOLE
1805-1881
Jamaican Nurse
HEROINE OF THE CRIMEAN WAR
lived here

The links still exist, due to the fact that many Jamaican families have members who settled in Britain in the 1950s, '60s, and '70s; however, recent restrictions on migration and the coming to light of abuses of the system have made getting visas

to stay in the UK nearly impossible, with the result that many now look at North America as a more attractive option.

MIGRATION

Despite their great love of their island, many Jamaicans have felt as strong a need to leave, frustrated by the lack of opportunity here and feeling that they would do better somewhere else. Wave after wave of the population have left for new lives abroad for economic reasons, and this has had a fracturing effect on the country's development, especially over the past five decades, as Jamaica moved from colonial to independent status.

The movement of Jamaicans to work in the cane fields of Cuba or on the construction of the Panama Canal continued through the early parts of the twentieth century, and some went as far afield as Costa Rica to work in banana cultivation and to the USA to look for work in South Florida as farm laborers. However, it was during the Second World War that a real change started, with Jamaicans and other West Indians leaving the islands to fight for King and country. After the war many chose to stay in the mother country, and Britain actively encouraged black workers to come and help rebuild it. This was the start of mass immigration to the UK, and a generation of Jamaicans left to start a new life in Western Europe. Many others left for America and Canada, and all these countries have a strong Jamaican diaspora that carries on the traditions of home. Despite visa restrictions that inhibit the travel of Jamaicans, there are areas in cities, such as Coldharbour Lane in Brixton, London, and Flatbush Avenue in Brooklyn, New York, that are synonymous with the island.

The feeling of needing to leave persists to this day. The lines outside the US Embassy in the sweltering sun in Kingston are a testimony to that. So why is it that people choose to leave the island, to "live in foreign," some never to return?

ATTITUDES TOWARD MONEY

Social mobility isn't easy in the Caribbean, and the divide between rich and poor is great. You'll often see a Range Rover and a pushcart battling for space on the streets of the capital. The rich of Kingston live in luxurious homes in the hills, literally looking down on the poor in the inner-city communities—a euphemism for the downtown ghettos. One thing that unites the people is their desire to improve their lot. Jamaicans, regardless of their social status and wealth, believe that they are worth more than they may actually have. For a middle-income developing country there are a lot of expensive vehicles on the road, with many people up to their eyeballs in debt to continue the illusion.

ATTITUDES TOWARD COLOR

The Jamaican motto, "Out of Many, One People," points to the diverse ethnic backgrounds that have come to symbolize the island as a melting pot. The reality is, however, that "class" and "color" are often interchangeable. The country has replaced one "C" with another, and, like any prejudice, it's hard to extinguish. It may be difficult to move classes, but having a fairer complexion will give you greater advantages in society because people's perceptions will be altered. In the past, during colonial times, certain jobs—such as front-of-house staff in banks and brokerage firms—would be given to white people. That attitude is still deep within the psyche of the people here, and skin bleaching products sell well across the country.

MACHO CULTURE

"A man is a man" in Jamaican society, which means he is the breadwinner, the head of the household, practical, strong-willed, sexually dominant, a good lover, with a wife and multiple girlfriends, and is probably a great driver, plumber, and all-around handyman. Anything else is viewed with suspicion, and any man who doesn't boast about his prowess in such matters is suspected of being gay—the last thing any male in Jamaica would want anyone to think. Even disagreeing with this kind of attitude in public, especially with regard to sexuality, will often lead people to assume that you must be gay yourself.

The country has a sizeable gay underground scene, but the newspapers, radio, and television feed the national preoccupation with homosexuality. The views of many are plain homophobic, and the more educated middle class tries to ignore it, with a "Don't ask, don't tell" attitude. Violence against gay people of both sexes, bisexuals, transvestites, and the transgendered is high, and is unlikely to be dissipated in the current climate.

chapter three

CUSTOMS & TRADITIONS

Religion plays a huge role in Jamaican society, the majority of the population being fervently Christian. Some groups follow traditional African religions, and there are communities of Jews, Hindus, and Muslims.

CHRISTIANITY

Jamaica has the highest number of churches per head of population in the world—take a trip anywhere on the island over the weekend and you'll soon believe it. You'll witness hundreds of people in their Sabbath best on their way to church, Bibles in hand, but it has to be remembered that the island's link to slavery is the key to the religious tradition seen here.

The Catholic Church dominates many islands in the Caribbean, but is less significant in Jamaica than in most of the region. The Spanish brought Catholicism to the island in the sixteenth century, but under the English it was banned in Jamaica until the last years of the eighteenth century. Today the Catholic Church has a far reach, socially and politically, despite its modest size. There have been a large number of Chinese converts to the faith, and the work of Father Richard Ho Lung, who in 1981 founded the Missionaries of the Poor—the first male religious order to be founded in the English-speaking Caribbean—has made a significant impact. The brothers work in downtown Kingston with the physically and mentally handicapped, and put on an annual musical production.

The Anglican Church, established in Jamaica in the seventeenth century, was dominated by the plantocracy, and in many respects was a party to slavery—some of the clergy spoke loudly in support of the planters and against emancipation, and some owned slaves. For many years the spiritual welfare of the enslaved received much the same treatment as their physical well-being—not much attention was paid. However, as other denominations began to convert slaves the Church's strength waned; this then changed the views of some of the slave owners, who saw the provision of religious guidance to slaves as a good thing, feeling a need for moral justification.

The Anglican diocese of Jamaica and the Cayman Islands was enormous, taking in also the Bahamas, British Honduras, and the Turks and Caicos Islands. By the mid-nineteenth century most of the other colonies had become separate dioceses.

The Anglicans have some of the most historic churches in Jamaica. They are found in the parish capitals across the island, and have been kept in generally good condition over the years.

Other popular denominations include the Baptists, who were instrumental in creating the first religious instruction that many of the slaves received, alongside the Moravians, and newer denominations such as the Church of God, Seventh-day Adventists, and Jehovah's Witnesses; all have sizeable congregations.

Services in many of the evangelical churches in Jamaica are much louder and go on much longer than those in other countries. They start early and finish late, with Sunday or Sabbath school lasting

much of the morning before the main event of the sermon, which can often last into the mid-afternoon. Visitors are very welcome and are encouraged to join in the services; Christ's command to "Go you therefore and teach all nations" is very much followed.

AFRICAN RELIGIONS

African religious traditions were allowed to thrive in Jamaica for many years because of the indifference of the planters toward their slaves. Their practices were carried to the New World, and the only attempt to stifle them was the banning of the drums that were an essential part of the worship. However, the enslaved Africans found ways of continuing to observe the faith they knew from home.

Kumina and Pocomania, commonly known as Poco, are two of the religions that were born out of the Great Revival of the 1860s. Both traditions are fusions of African practices, which had been banned in slavery, with European religious influences. Between 1841 and 1865 a new wave of around eight thousand Africans came from West and parts of Central Africa to Jamaica as indentured workers, and brought their faith with them. They settled in the east of the island

around the parish of St. Thomas, and this area still has the strongest adherents.

Believers in Poco hold their meetings at "Balm yards." A tall bamboo pole is used to mark the revival ground where meetings are held. The rituals involve rhythmic drumming and "chupping," a form of breathing or hyperventilating that sends the worshipers spinning counterclockwise into a trance, where they often speak in tongues, the translation often given by the leader, known as the "Shepherd," or "Mother," if a woman. The services are exciting: the congregation sings uplifting choruses accompanied by tambourines and drums, and worshipers in colored, turban-style head wraps dance and spin around each other.

Kumina is probably the most African of Jamaica's religious traditions. Its name comes from two Ashanti Twi words from Ghana: *akom*, to be possessed, and *ana*, by an ancestor. The faith is based on ancestor worship, in which spirits of the dead, called "duppies," are either appeased or brought in to help with life on earth. In Kumina ceremonies the drum plays a key part of the service, as do spirit possession and animal sacrifice.

Obeah is what most people would class as Jamaica's version of voodoo, a type of black magic. The word *obeah* is again a mix of Ashanti words: *obi*, child, and *yi*, take. Its dark nature has seen Obeah banned since slave days, but a quick look in the paper will still see ads from practitioners offering solutions to a wide variety of problems. Myal is the name given to a form of Obeah used for good.

The practices of Kumina, Poco, and Obeah were once very popular, but today most people on the island would be hard-pressed to distinguish between the different forms.

RASTAFARI

This faith, which has played a part in making Jamaica known across the globe, is its most recent and noticeable religion. The red, gold, and green that has become symbolic of Rastas has become advertising shorthand for island life, as have also the Rastafari dreadlocks and the Lion of Judah, one of the regal titles of their God, Haile Selassie, the last Emperor of Ethiopia.

Rastafarianism came out of the Black Nationalism preached by Marcus Garvey and the Universal Negro Improvement Association that he founded in 1914. He proclaimed that the poor and disenfranchised black people in the diaspora should look to Africa, where a black king would be crowned, for the day of deliverance was at hand.

That moment for many came in 1930 when Ras (an honorific title similar to Duke or Prince) Tafari Makonnen was crowned Emperor of Abyssinia and became Haile Selassie I. Garvey is regarded by Rastafari as a prophet for  his vision that salvation from oppression would come from African unity, in the shape of the only independent black monarch on the continent.

Early believers looked to the Book of Revelation for signs that the crowning of Haile Selassie was the second coming, and that he was the incarnation of God known as Jah. His claim to be a direct descendant of King Solomon and the Queen of Sheba supported his titles of King of Kings, Lord of Lords, and the Conqueror Lion of the Tribe of Judah.

A number of Jamaicans who had been living abroad returned to the island in the early 1930s and

started to preach and teach the message of
Rastafari. They were recognizable by their long
hair, matted into dreadlocks in emulation of the
Lion of Judah and the biblical sect of Nazarenes,
who grew their hair and did not cut it.

Leonard Howell, who has been described as
"the first Rasta," also became the first to be
persecuted, charged with sedition for declaring
allegiance to Haile Selassie and not to the King of
England, George V. He was jailed, but on his
release he formed the first commune, Pinnacle, an
abandoned Great House in St. Catherine, which at
its height had more than two thousand followers.

Persecution became a routine occurrence for
followers of the faith, as in the early days its
tenets were strongly antiwhite. In the British
colonial era, the idea of a faith that fostered a
hatred of whites, preached that Africans were
God's chosen people and would eventually rule
the world, and encouraged black people to
believe that white people would one day be their
servants, was more than revolutionary, and
needed to be put down. Pinnacle was regularly
raided and its members arrested—and once
locked up they had their dreads shorn from their
heads. This happened so many times that
eventually those followers who were left started
new communities in Kingston.

Slowly but surely, the message of Rastafari
gained momentum. The Rastafari were associated
with the "Blackheart Man," in reference to an
evildoer, and for a long time this was an image

that stuck, but the emergence of reggae music has transformed Rastafari in the eyes of many. Rastafarianism is, however, perhaps surprisingly, looked down on in some quarters in Jamaica.

Rasta Rituals
The Bingi

"Reasonings" are informal sessions where Rastafari come together to commune and discuss a wide range of issues. Great occasions, such as the birthday and crowning of His Imperial Majesty Haile Selassie, will see much bigger formal gatherings, known as "Grounations" or "Nyabingis," named after the drums used alongside the chants and prayers. The preparations for these large outdoor events can start days in advance, and they'll often carry on for just as long. These mass events often bring together Rastas from across the island, and sometimes involve feasts. The smell of the large wood fire that can always be found at these events, mixed with ganja and the lemongrass used to scent the Tabernacle—the large thatched building that houses the altar, drums, and orchestra—is quite an experience. Before lighting the fire a prayer is said: "Glory be to the father and to the maker of creation. As it was in the beginning is now and ever shall be, World without end: Jah Rastafari: Eternal God Selassie I."

Ganja was first introduced to Jamaica by Indian indentured laborers, who brought marijuana with them. It soon became popular, but was made illegal shortly after its introduction because employers found it slowed down the work rate. For Rastafari ganja is a holy herb and an essential part of the faith. It is a sacrament that is used to enable Rastas to gain insight and commune with God. The smokers pass the spliff (more commonly known as scliff) or a chalice (a big ganja pipe) clockwise around the group.

The wearing of dreadlocks is very closely associated with the movement, though not universal among, or exclusive to, its adherents. "You don't hafi dread to be Rasta," as the song by

Morgan Heritage says. Many people who have Rasta leanings don't always wear dreads but support the faith in other ways. Those who wear locks but aren't Rasta are looked down on as imposters by Rasta and nonbelievers alike. In parts of the diaspora wearing dreads is seen as a sign of black consciousness or a visible sign of nonconformity; however, in Jamaica the struggle that Rastafari has been through means that most people who wear the locks are believers and live by the doctrines laid out.

Food Laws

Rastafarians eat strictly Ital, or I-tal, which means natural and clean. This excludes scavengers, shellfish, and meat, especially pork. Vegetables make up the key part of the diet, which is to all intents and purposes vegan.

NATIONAL HOLIDAYS

January 1	New Year's Day
February	Ash Wednesday
March/April	Good Friday
March/April	Easter Monday
May 23	Labour Day
August 1	Emancipation Day
August 6	Independence Day
Mid-October	National Heroes' Day
December 25	Christmas Day
December 26	Boxing Day

Good Friday (March/April)

Many families get together and attend church. Traditionally fish and bread were prepared beforehand and eaten the following day after fasting on Good Friday.

In rural areas it is believed that cutting the physic nut tree on Good Friday will yield a reddish fluid, symbolizing the blood of Christ. Some also believe that the tree is similar to that used in the crucifixion.

Easter Monday (March/April)

Kite festivals are common around the island. People take homemade kites and fly them for show, or even fight with them, having aerial battles to cut the string of the opponent.

The Easter weekend also sees the Trelawny Yam Festival, one of the key local food events on the island.

Labour Day (May 23)

During the colonial period, this was Empire Day, and Queen Victoria's Birthday, but since 1961 it has marked the day Alexander Bustamante led a labor rebellion that helped to usher in independence. Since the 1970s it has been more about helping to build the nation. People help their elderly neighbors and engage in community work, such as painting fences, collecting garbage, and sprucing up their area.

Emancipation Day (August 1)

Known as Augus Mawnin, this date commemorates August 1, 1838, when slavery on the island was finally abolished. Now the country holds events across the island to mark that momentous occasion.

Independence Day (August 6)

The country is full of black, gold, and green, from flags to face paint, as people celebrate the day in 1962 when the island ended its colonial history and started out on its independent status. Now there is a Grand Parade through the streets of the capital, Kingston, with costumed performers and vintage cars. Other cultural events include the Grand Gala, held at the National Stadium, and street dances in celebration across the island.

National Heroes Day (mid-October)
This day honors the ancestors who helped to shape the country.

Christmas Eve (December 24)
One tradition in most towns is "Christmas Walking Out," when people promenade around the squares and streets on Christmas Eve. Families gather around dusk and go window-shopping and wishing the season's greetings to friends and strangers alike, until late into the evening. It's one of the rare occasions when stores and shops stay open quite late to allow people to buy last-minute presents.

Christmas Day (December 25)
On the day itself food is an essential part of the festivities, and can include curried goat, pork, oxtail, and chicken, all served with rice and gungo peas. For the Christmas cake fruits are soaked in red wine and white rum for months, and juice made from sorrel is drunk.

JAMAICAN TRADITIONS
With religion playing such a major role in the lives of many Jamaicans, it's not surprising that the more personal events or rites of passage such as weddings and, especially, funerals have a strong element of faith running through them. It's in the rituals of death that one of the most distinctive elements of Jamaica's African past is celebrated nearly universally.

Nine Nights

Nine Nights is, as the name suggests, a celebration that lasts for nine days after someone's death. The friends and family of the deceased will gather at their home, known as the "dead yard," and reminisce every evening over food and drink and singing. The final evening or "setup" is more like a party, with libations or offerings of alcohol poured or thrown from open bottles or glasses on to the ground.

The mood of the evening is uplifting, with sound systems, dancing, dominoes, and stories about the life of the deceased. A table of food is left out for the spirit of the departed, which cannot be touched until after midnight, the time when the spirit makes the passage from this world to the next.

Jonkanoo

Rarely seen nowadays, the masquerade tradition still scares those who encounter it. Dressed up as characters such as the Cow Head, the Hobby Horse, the Wild Indian, and the Devil, performers run around the streets, especially at Christmas, and on national holidays such as Emancipation Day. You'll see young men and teenage boys in ghoulish costumes and masks; they'll surround drivers in their cars, and chase young children. It's a real spectacle—one that goes back generations—and those involved will stretch out a hand for donations after they've performed. Like many of the traditions on the island, it's believed to be of West African origin.

CARNIVAL

Carnival is celebrated throughout the region, and Jamaica is no exception. It isn't as popular as the Carnivals of Trinidad and the other islands in the eastern Caribbean. Soca and calypso are not widely listened to, as Jamaica's music is reggae and dancehall, but from a small start back in 1990 it has grown.

The brainchild of Jamaican calypso star Byron Lee, Carnival has become a cultural highlight in the calendar. The entire month starts around Lent, in February, and sees parties or Bacchanal every weekend at Mas Camp—a purpose-built outdoor venue in Kingston that hosts the latest sounds and top international acts.

The grand finale is a street parade, or "Road March," around the capital with people dressed up, sometimes in outrageous costumes. There are also events in Montego Bay and Boscobel, the home of Beach Jovert, where participants throw paint at each other and drink and dance to soca by the sea. Carnival, and indeed soca and calypso, have always been more associated with uptown than downtown, and the class division is still an issue.

The revealing costumes were the subject of a national debate over morality in music, with many dancehall deejays questioning why their music and videos were banned from television while the carnival was being broadcast live and uncensored as people young and old "wine"— gyrate to the music, which is also laced with innuendo.

GOOD AND BAD LUCK OMENS

Jamaica is a very superstitious country: the folklore of the island runs deep within the national psyche. Many of the beliefs and practices are African traditions that have survived slavery, but the exact reasons for them are long forgotten. The customs permeate people's everyday lives, and are used for many purposes and in many circumstances—from advice offered to strangers to gambling tips for those hoping to strike it rich in the lotto.

- If you wish to know the depth of the love someone feels for you, make a few knots in a thread and place a flame over it. If the flame passes over the knots, the love is strong.

- If anything is broken during a wedding reception, the marriage will be unhappy.

- If you dream about new shoes, you will have a new lover. If you dream about a wedding, there will be a funeral. If you dream about a new house, there will be a death.

- The umbilical cord of a newborn baby must not be allowed to fall on the floor. It must be guarded by the mother and buried in the ground between three days and a year after the birth. A tree should be planted in that spot, known as the child's navel string tree, and if it is damaged or destroyed the child must be compensated. If the property is sold a new tree must be planted for the child from a sucker of the original tree.

- A baby born during a leap year will be lucky.

- A baby boy who resembles his mother will be lucky, as will a baby girl who resembles her father.

- If you say that an infant is beautiful, he will grow ugly. If you say he is ugly, he will grow handsome.

- Birthmarks are caused during pregnancy. If the mother scratches her body when she has a food craving the baby will be born with a mark on that place, often in the shape of the food the mother craved.

- White rum is often used in folk beliefs; some say that it wards off evil spirits. Rum is thrown on the ground around the area marked out for a new home to bring good luck to the owner and its inhabitants and to provide protection for the workers.

- People will splash a few drops of rum on the ground for good luck, especially when they are about to gamble at the track or at the shop when playing lotto; others say it can fend off "duppy" ghosts.

chapter four

MAKING FRIENDS

For most Jamaicans, the friends made at school are the most enduring. The children they "ramp" with, or play with, in their early years will often be the friends who remain throughout their lives. Also, relatives of around the same age, especially if they have grown up in the same district or community, will often remain very close. It is not uncommon for cousins, nephews, nieces, brothers, and sisters all to be raised by a grandmother, and these family ties may be the strongest of all.

It can take a while for outsiders to create a bond that can come anywhere near those created by time and shared experience. However, when it happens, a friendship with a Jamaican will last a lifetime. The visitor to Jamaica can make such a friendship, but it will take much longer than a two-week vacation. Business relationships may be more likely to lead to friendships, as they may bring more chances to interact socially outside a working environment.

A Jamaican friend will also be able to help you negotiate everyday transactions. To get ahead in Jamaica it really is who you know, not what you know, that counts, and when you come up against red tape and petty bureaucracy a close Jamaican friend will be invaluable. They'll help you avoid the "tourist tax" (inflated shop prices for tourists) that every foreigner will experience at some point or other, and they'll protect you in ways you may not even realize, from guiding you along the street to stop you from falling into a gully to standing up for you in arguments (the scene of a Jamaican tongue-lashing is a sight to behold).

Most people are proud of their country and believe it to be the best, but those from the "Rock" will go out of their way to show you a side of the island that is much more beautiful than the beaches and azure seas in the travel brochures.

WHO'S GENUINE?

Jamaicans are genuinely friendly. However, the fear of crime means that getting to know people can be tricky, and social inequality also plays a part. It's easy to see possible ulterior motives behind many of the interactions you will have, especially away from a work or professional setting, from the friendly taxi man who tries to get you into his minivan with a poor imitation of an American accent to the chirpy craft market vendor who kisses his teeth—a common Jamaican expression of disdain—when you politely refuse to buy a carved wooden head. Eventually even the smiling face in the hotel lobby starts to be seen in a slightly different way. Don't let that put you off, however. Unlike many other places, the directness of Jamaicans is actually a refreshing change as the pretense of friendliness in some is apparent immediately, and the warmth you'll receive from others, especially in more rural parts of the country, is completely different from the images that are portrayed in the media. If you're driving in the country and you're in a pickup, don't be surprised if someone asks for a lift. They'll just hop up in the back and jump out when they get to their destination. In the countryside people are ready to open themselves up to strangers, as in many cases they live so far off the beaten track that your visit will be spoken of for days. The sense of national pride is at its greatest when Jamaicans can show you the beauty of the place because you've made the effort to take a look.

MEETING PEOPLE

It'll generally be casual acquaintances that you'll make, and such connections are easy to make as a foreigner. People will often come up to you, and engage in chitchat on the street, or offer to help with directions, or take you on a tour—wanted or not. Also, Jamaicans love to socialize, and the country, with its tropical climate, is ideally suited to cooling out (hanging out). From the busiest of the inner-city communities to the most rural village there will be a central spot where people can be found of an evening playing dominoes, eating, drinking, or dancing—or all of the above.

People will probably be a little inquisitive about you and what you think of the island. Jamaicans are very proud of the country, so be complimentary—a list of negatives wouldn't go over well.

Chatting to people is easy in the clubs of Negril, Montego Bay, and Kingston. Here you'll often find people—both men and women—who will welcome you into their group. Just be yourself, and you'll blend in. Jamaicans don't take kindly to show-offs and bigheads who flaunt their wealth. You'll also be more likely to meet hustlers in this setting than anywhere else, but if you go in prepared you'll have fun.

For visitors staying in the country for a longer period, joining associations, from the Jamaica Georgian Society to the Rotarians, and social groups, including church groups, can be great ways of meeting people.

GREETINGS
Formal and informal greetings in Jamaica depend on familiarity. A normal handshake is appropriate

in most settings, but Jamaican women will hug male and female friends. Men will generally bump fists and often add a joint cross of the thumbs—a common greeting between Rastafari that has become standard among Jamaicans. Rasta talk has also found its way into other verbal greetings, such as "bredren," "sisdrin," in reference to male and female friends, and "Bless up," "Wha gwan?" and "Respect" are common expressions.

TIMEKEEPING

People in Jamaica often talk about "Jamaican time"—a reference to the slightly fluid attitude to timekeeping that exists on the island. Making an arrangement can be a tricky business, as more often than not people will arrive quite late at social events, the cell phone now providing an easy way of keeping in touch and making excuses. In a business setting, however, being late, especially as a foreigner, is frowned upon, as you will be expected to have better manners.

GIFT GIVING

Jamaicans who can give will do so—it's a long-standing tradition that continues to this day. Labour Day in Jamaica really is just that, with friends coming together to help the elderly in the area in various ways, ranging from bushing (trimming) lawns to mending clothes and cutting hair. You'll also see people on the streets painting road markings, sweeping, and generally showing community spirit.

Jamaicans abroad have a Christmas tradition of sending gifts home, packed in cardboard barrels. Every year the wharves and ports of Jamaica are packed full of these barrels waiting to be cleared through customs. They are filled with nonperishable items such as canned food, clothes, shoes, and anything else that isn't easily available in the country. This tradition started back in the political turmoil of the 1970s, when everyday items weren't coming into the island, or the prices if they were available were beyond the average person's pocketbook. Family members "in foreign"— abroad—would send items collected over the course of the year back to their relatives. The custom still continues, with families looking forward to their barrels at Christmas. Now the cost of shipping, however, has seen more and more people move toward sending money via remittance agents instead. When a barrel does come, everyone gets something, including neighbors and friends. It's an opportunity to show off the largesse of the person who has "gone to foreign."

It's been remarked by sociologists on the island that Jamaica now has a generation of "barrel children"—kids raised by grandparents or other family members who are sustained via the gifts sent back to them by parents working abroad. There are concerns that not only does this have a destabilizing effect on the family structure on the island, but it also creates a dependence mentality in the nation's young—that things are given rather than earned.

Gifts are also expected when people return to the island. Sit in a foreign airport and watch a flight departing for Kingston or Montego Bay, and see the pandemonium as people load, unload, and hastily repack suitcases that are overweight, but all trying to squeeze in that last item for an aunty or cousin to help them out. The international carriers must make a fortune with excess baggage charges on flights to JA.

BEGGING

As you travel around as a foreigner, you'll at some point be asked for money. It isn't demeaning in Jamaica to ask for assistance, and it's become an accepted part of life. Those who have, give to the have-nots. However, as someone who lives abroad you have more than the average person, so you can expect to be asked quite a few times. Those who "beg a money" range from the street people, who will often be using the money to feed a drug addiction, to people passing you on the road who may have to "buy a pampers" for their child or who "need bus fare." The reasons given may vary, and the response if you don't give can equally vary. Some people will be good-natured, but others can get quite angry, depending on how you refuse. As we have seen, "respect" is key in Jamaican society, and some people will get quite heated if they feel that they've been "dissed," or slighted.

PHOTOGRAPHY

Jamaicans love to have their picture taken. Spot a group of girls with a camera, and the level of posing would not seem out of place on a fashion shoot. However, like many places in the world, asking permission of your subject is especially advised in Jamaica. Not only is it common courtesy, but some people are very suspicious of being photographed—they really might not want to be on film, or on somebody's laptop. Even taking a shot of a building with people in the foreground can be problematic and can easily lead to arguments. If you do take someone's portrait in the street, be prepared to give them "a little something"—some money for their time.

INVITATIONS HOME

You are unlikely to be invited to someone's home in Jamaica unless you are already quite friendly with them. It would be surprising, for example, to be invited to the home of a work colleague; as in many countries, work life and home life are very separate, and people don't like crossing the divide. On a Sunday people will often cook a little extra in case a visitor comes over, but, again, it's unlikely that the person would be from work.

If you are invited you won't be expected to bring any wine or spirits, but if you know your hosts drink a bottle would be appreciated. Dress on the smarter side of casual, as Jamaicans would take it as an insult if you showed up at their home looking as if you hadn't made an effort (and it would certainly be noticed). Jamaicans, male and female, take great pride in their cooking and so inviting guests is a chance for them to impress, among people they feel comfortable with, even if it's food prepared by a helper. Jamaicans will feed you well—it would be rude not to.

Arrive soon after the time set, as most people won't expect you to be right on time. They will, however, expect you to be more punctual than their local guests, who might be half an hour late for a dinner or as much as two or three hours late for a barbecue!

It depends on the group, but someone's home is one place where people can generally talk about politics. The conversation can easily move on to sex—and that will be very tongue in cheek—but try to avoid talking about atheism, drug use, or homosexuality. Many social occasions in Jamaica last well into the night, but when going to people's homes expect to end the visit a bit earlier, so around midnight or 1:00 a.m. is a good time to call it a night.

SOCIALIZING WITH THE OPPOSITE SEX

Very open attitudes mean that it is easy to meet and go out with someone of the opposite sex. Pretty much everywhere you'll see men and women flirting. Actually, it's more direct than flirting—it can often be an out-and-out proposal. Some people find this a refreshing change, but others can find the persistence of would-be partners annoying. A playful dismissal is all that's needed to ward off most approaches.

The dancehalls and stage shows are places where approaches may leave nothing to the imagination. Most men and women meet at clubs rather than bars, which are still mainly for men. The gyrating and grinding of dancing bodies lead many women to position themselves against the wall, as if they're even slightly exposed a man might try to squeeze in behind them for a quick grind against a backside.

As a foreigner in some of the tourist areas you'll be asked to dance. This is often innocent, but there are large numbers of sex workers who operate from the clubs of Negril, Montego Bay, and Ocho Rios.

FAMILY LIFE

The family is important to Jamaicans. The structure in many cases is matriarchal, going back to the days of slavery. Under the chattel system men were seen as breeding stock, and families would often be split up and sold. The traditional patriarchal family found in West Africa soon became a thing of the past for their descendants living in the Caribbean.

A common situation now is that a single woman raises a number of children, with the extended family, particularly the grandparents, playing a key part in their upbringing—a role many understand, having themselves been raised in a similar way.

A couple might have several children from previous relationships of both the man and the woman. The men in these families are either the "baby father," who is providing for his own child or children, or a new partner. A number of half- and step-siblings can lead to many people living under one roof.

A joke from a popular Jamaican pantomime sums up a common situation. "What is DNA?"

asks one character. "Daddy not available," the other replies. In Jamaica, "minding," or raising, another man's child, knowingly or otherwise, is a common scenario. The fear of infidelity, of his partner "giving bun," or cheating with other men, is so great that there is a growing trend for men to take DNA tests, to try to ensure that the child they are calling their own isn't a "jacket" claiming their name.

There are, of course, the traditional nuclear families, found mostly in the middle classes and more religious homes.

The gender role stereotypes are firmly ingrained in Jamaican society: the man is the breadwinner, and the woman is the homemaker and child rearer. It is expected that a man will try to fulfill his role, but  economic constraints in the society have made it difficult for many. A man who fails in this is often seen as "wotless," or worthless, regardless of the difficulties he may have in finding employment.

FAMILY OCCASIONS

Within the Jamaican family, social events often involve coming together to see elderly relatives, with reunions a common occurrence on the island.

Relatives may meet up once a year to celebrate familial ties that may have been strained by time and distance, but are repaired over curry goat, rice and peas, and white rum.

The key family occasions in Jamaica are much the same as everywhere in the world. You're expected to join in the festivities. Don't be so wild that you make a spectacle of yourself and become an embarrassment, but do get involved!

Birth

The birth of a baby sees the parents with relatives and friends attending church to see the newborn blessed or christened. Such services take place nearly every Saturday or Sunday morning in Jamaica. Even if people are not regular attenders this event is very important within the society. Friends are expected to bring a gift, and the parents often have a gathering in the evening to celebrate the occasion.

Weddings

Weddings see months of effort that seemingly involve everybody. People chip in where they can to help out. Friends and family will be pressed for connections that can be used for cutting the cost of anything from venues to a good pastor and florist, and may even be drafted in to cook on the day. The ceremony will include the kind of sermon that is generally used by the minister to preach to a new flock, including both the saved and unsaved regular churchgoers, and occasional attenders.

There are two particular wedding traditions that are common in Jamaica: the unveiling of the cake, and the removal of the bride's garter, which the groom does with his teeth as she sits on a chair. It's harmless if rather risqué fun.

Funerals

A funeral in Jamaica is a grand social affair—a celebration of life that often brings people from near and far to reflect on the recently departed. Drinking and dominoes see people gathering for many days before the funeral as people cook up food and mourn; friends, family, and strangers gather to provide support.

DAILY LIFE

Most people in Jamaica rise early, to start the day soon after daybreak, regardless of whether they live in the city or the country. The sun rises shortly after 6:00 a.m. in the height of summer, and around 7:00 a.m. in winter. People prefer to get their housework done early, because it gets too hot later in the day. Eating breakfast together as a family is common, especially when there are young children, before they make their way to school via route taxi or minibus.

The traditional school run found in other countries is rare in Jamaica. Some people may do the daily drop-off, especially the middle classes, and others may pay to make sure their child gets picked up by a regular taxi driver, but around the island many children from an early age make the journey themselves. Every school day you'll see regular minibuses and route taxis that run along the main roads between the towns and villages full of pupils. The drivers take lower fares, but there has been controversy about some operators and their "ductors" (conductors) taking advantage of teenage girls and of inappropriate music and behavior onboard the buses.

Many people live away from the main population centers in small communities that require multiple taxis, and for those making the minimum wage, such as household domestics, the cost of commuting can be nearly half their salary of about $40 dollars a week. Another expense is lunch; most people will buy a "box lunch" in a styrofoam container from the many street vendors or "cook shops" that sell hot food. Many adults and children, especially those in a rush, will grab a patty—a Jamaican-style pastry filled with chicken, fish, or soybean, and vegetables. Children at home and at school love snacks—the

supermarkets have row upon row of cheesy wheat products, peanuts, chocolates, and sweets. A sit-down meal generally consists of some meat—mostly chicken—some side salad—often coleslaw— and always rice.

Having lunch out is common, but the evening meal is nearly always eaten at home with family or friends. The combination of the fear of crime and a lack of entertainment options outside the main population centers, plus the fact that the days are long and there are only two free-to-air TV channels, means that many people go to bed early.

Good, well-paid jobs are in short supply in Jamaica. This gives employers the upper hand, and despite strong labor laws many workers feel they don't have much power. With unemployment at around 10 percent, and with a high cost of living, many Jamaicans are constantly looking for work or for a better-paid job.

Buying and selling informally is the only employment for many. You'll see "higglers" at the side of the road and in the markets selling a wide variety of goods, from cell phone chargers and car accessories to fruit and vegetables. Lots of people keep small shops stocking the basics and other essential items, such as phone cards, for people who live nearby. There are supermarkets in most towns that stock a wider variety of goods, but if specialty items are needed there are a few high-end supermarkets in Kingston, Montego Bay, and Mandeville that are popular with the more well-heeled.

GROWING UP IN JAMAICA
Children

Jamaican families in the past tended to be large, with high infant mortality rates. Nowadays the family size is smaller, but "outside" children (children born outside formal relationships) are high in number. Nearly a third of Jamaica's population is below the age of fifteen.

The rough-and-tumble nature of the society sees children behaving more like adults at a very young age. They'll often take on responsibilities such as regular household chores, caring for younger siblings, and in some cases selling goods on the street. They have no choice, because of the economic situation of their parents.

You'll often see kids going unaccompanied down to the store, and crossing busy roads at a much younger age than you'd see in more developed nations. This creates a maturity in young Jamaican children, and one might feel that they've grown up a bit too quickly. However, you'll also see, in poorer rural areas, scenes from another era—children playing marbles on a dirt road, building kites out of string and bits of discarded plastic, shooting birds with catapults, and catching lizards, basically enjoying a childhood long gone in many other parts of the world.

Education

The country has achieved a basic literacy rate of 80 percent, but research has shown that only 64 percent have functional literacy—the ability to understand complex ideas and documents. Many people want more investment in education to counter the effects of high unemployment, an underskilled workforce, and low productivity.

Enrollment in preschool in Jamaica is one of the largest in the region, with more than 2,500 early childhood centers on the island for children aged between one and six. Seeing a group of children graduating to primary school would make many high-school seniors in the USA feel inferior. The children are turned out immaculately for the event, the girls in white dresses and the boys in white shirts, black trousers, and good shoes. It's clear that education is still a big deal on the island, although, as we have seen, many young parents today attach less importance to it.

Tuition is now free in Jamaica, the JLP (Jamaica Labor Party) having removed fees in 2007 for children between the ages of five and eleven at primary school and between eleven and sixteen at secondary school. However, not everything is free, and some parents now pay more in other costs than they did before, as schools try to keep money coming in. In some cases extracurricular activities have had to be cut, as parents and school budgets cannot fund them. The cost of books, uniforms, lunch, and transportation makes sending

children to school prohibitive for some parents, but many make sacrifices to pay for such things and get their children through school.

At the age of eleven, students take exams to determine which secondary school they will attend. The Grade Six Achievement Test, or GSAT, is a source of great stress for parents, teachers, and especially pupils, across the country. Students choose five secondary schools, and based on their results they are placed in a school of their choice.

At secondary schools students aged sixteen take their Caribbean Examination Council (CXC) Caribbean Secondary Education Certificate, and if they progress to the sixth form their CAPE (Caribbean Advanced Proficiency Exams). These are the equivalent of the GCSE and A Level examinations in the United Kingdom.

The education that pupils get is structured and disciplined. It more closely resembles the way children were taught during Jamaica's colonial era nearly fifty years ago than the British system now. Children learn a lot by rote, but have a deeper understanding of subjects at an earlier age. The use of corporal punishment is not allowed by teachers in class—only the head teacher is allowed to use it in certain situations—however its use is an ongoing debate in the country. There have been some serious cases that have prompted moves to ban its use in the country completely.

Children all wear school uniform, and the dress code is strictly enforced (though boys like to wear their khaki shirts outside their trousers and their ties short). In school pupils will be told off for trying to break the dress rules, and may be punished. In the street you may see pupils trying to look casual and "cool," and the police and even members of the general public will castigate these "schoolers," as they are known, and tell them to pull their pants up and tuck their shirts in. They'll also tell them to head home, especially if they are just hanging  around. The view is that no good can come of children doing nothing when they should be doing homework.

Every year the nation's students battle it out physically rather than academically at Champs, one of the biggest school sports days in the world. Thousands of athletes who hope to be the next big thing challenge each other to be that big thing—the next Asafa Powell, Usain Bolt, Veronica Campbell Brown, or Shelly Ann Fraser.

They also battle it out academically, on television. The longest-running TV show in Jamaica is the "Schools Challenge Quiz," in which teams of four

pupils take part in round after round of grueling general knowledge questions. Spelling bees are also very popular, so much so that the first non-American winner of the internationally renowned Scripps Spelling Bee in the

USA was Jamaican born, raised, and trained.

Higher education in Jamaica sees a wide cross-section of the island's youth applying to the two main universities on the island—the University of the West Indies at Mona, and Utech in Papine. The two campuses in Kingston are rivals, but the reputation of UWI and its much wider Caribbean intake make it the more prestigious of the two. Once students finish their degrees many leave the country because of a lack of opportunities and for better pay. This brain drain is having a serious domino effect on the island's development.

Youth Culture
Because of the fact that children and teenagers are a significantly large section of society, youth culture

is evident everywhere, such as in the dancehall music that is heard around the island, and even in the way that older people dress more youthfully than in many other parts of the world. Young and old still party together at dances—something that adds to the youthfulness of the island.

The youth culture in other parts of the West is now very similar to that of Jamaica. The music and style of Jamaican immigrants has influenced the street style of inner cities in the Americas and Europe. Even the way many young people talk and dress, especially in London, Manchester, New York, and Toronto, has been shaped by the fashions of the Caribbean.

HEALTH SERVICES

Jamaica trains many of the doctors in the Caribbean at the University of the West Indies, and thousands of the island's doctors and nurses have left to work in the USA, Canada, and the UK. They are a severe loss, and medical facilities in the country's public sector can barely cope with local demand.

The standards of care in the hospitals around the country vary. There are smaller facilities in the parish capitals, but the best are the University Hospital of the West Indies, Kingston, Kingston Public Hospital (KPH), and Cornwall Regional Hospital in Montego Bay. There are a number of private clinics across the country. There are pharmacists in most small towns carrying generic and brand-name drugs.

The Jamaica Labour Party, when elected in 2007, abolished end-user fees for patients. Before that, if people fell ill and went to the doctor or hospital they could in some cases be refused care if they didn't have the money. The access to free health care for all has unfortunately overburdened the country's already overworked and under-resourced hospitals and clinics, and there are long waiting lists for all surgical procedures. Private health care on the island or in the USA is the preferred option for those who can afford it.

HOUSING

Most Jamaicans now live close to the urban centers for work. Kingston has been the main draw, but May Pen, Mandeville, Montego Bay, Ocho Rios, and some of the old regional capitals have the largest populations. In the past, most people built wooden board houses—these were cheap and easy to construct—or wattle and daub homes, which were cooler than brick. Now, however, nearly all building is done with cement blocks, and as you drive through the country you will gain a lasting image of numerous buildings at various stages of completion. The types of housing vary, especially in Kingston—some of the infamous inner-city ghettos or garrisons there have well-built two-story block homes and high-rise apartments, but a few streets away it's all zinc fences and roofs and wooden board houses. Further uptown, in areas that sound upscale, such as Skyline Drive, Norwood, Cherry Gardens, Stony Hill, and the grand Beverley Hills, multiroom mansions and town houses abound.

"Building a house" is a dream for most Jamaicans—buying a plot of land and constructing a home is what most people do. Jamaica is often seen as one of the property bargains of the Caribbean, but the cost of buying and building a house is still high for most people, and there is widespread squatting as people "capture" land. The government has sought to regulate the situation as around a third of the population lives in these predominantly rural communities that range from wooden board houses to

quite grand concrete structures. The squatting communities have been blamed in some quarters for the spread of crime around the island. The sense of knowing your neighbors that exists in more settled and affluent communities is absent in some squatting sites, where new faces may come and go all the time. Criminals escaping from one urban area to another have been known to hide out in squatting communities and eventually add to the crime problem in their adopted city. Living in these communities can also have a negative effect on those trying to get work—if their addresses and areas are synonymous with the poorer parts of society, employers often won't give them a chance.

chapter six

TIME OUT

Jamaicans enjoy their leisure time. The range of things to do may be limited, and the cost prohibitive, but because the pace of life is slower people tend just to make the most of their free time around family, social gatherings, and the church. Most people in the 1.1 million who make up the workforce don't work on weekends, and those in regular employment are entitled to two weeks' paid vacation a year. There are also the various public holidays, which are either religious or of national significance.

The beach is a popular hangout on weekends, with church groups and families congregating at "local beaches," as expats call them, such as Hellshire Beach in St. Catherine.

EATING OUT AND EATING IN

Jamaica has an abundance of "cook shops"— takeouts that sell a wide variety of local dishes. These are generally "no frills" eateries, ranging from an improvised barbecue on a shopping cart, using an old steel wheel piled with charcoal as a grill, to a hole-in-the-wall venue with a table and a few plastic chairs.

Because of the vegetarian diet of Rastafari there are always good choices for "Ital" food (very similar to vegan without salt) available in most busy towns. All the fast-food giants are here too, and are very popular—that is, all except McDonald's. The world's largest fast-food chain opened franchises on the island but was unsuccessful, so back in 2005 they left, despite having spent millions on their investment. It seems that the Jamaican public just didn't buy into the brand, and fierce competition from the various patty shops didn't help. The Jamaican patty is a flaky pastry that contains various fillings, such as chicken, fish, or soybean, with vegetables and spices, and is often tinted golden yellow with egg yolk or turmeric. It is made like a turnover, but is more savory, and is an institution in itself. The competition between the various outlets—Mother's, Tastee, and Juci—is fierce.

Eating out at high-end restaurants with international cuisine is a hit-and-miss affair and well beyond the pocketbooks of the average Jamaican. In the more tourist-oriented towns the options are much better, but the catering industry hasn't developed as much as it might because of the all-inclusive package grip on the tourist dollar—many vacationers rarely leave their hotels, in part because meals are included in their package holidays. However, restaurants in Kingston are frequented by both locals and expatriates and there are a number of places where you can experience fine dining, although the prices are very high. Most Jamaicans eat at home, and invite friends and family to gatherings, especially on weekends.

The country may be relatively small, but some parts of the island have developed food specialties that have to be tried. Jamaican jerk cooking—in which meats are dry rubbed or marinated with a very hot spice mixture called Jamaican jerk spice—was invented by the maroons, those descendants of slaves who escaped during the

Spanish occupation and subsequent runaways, who lived in the interior of the island. It's found across the island, but Boston Bay in Portland on the east coast is well-known for its jerk chicken and pork. Shrimp, conch, and seafood in general are available at Little Ochie, on the south coast. The many nations that have contributed to Jamaica's diversity have also added to the island's tastes, with African, Indian, Chinese, Lebanese, Syrian, English, and German influences.

DRINKING

Bars—especially the rum shops serving the strong white rum that is almost universally drunk because of its low price and high alcohol content—are male dominated, but nearly all have female bartenders. The banter in these places tends to be quite loud and boisterous, and there's generally a social stigma attached to women who frequent bars, especially if they come in on their own, although there are many women bar owners.

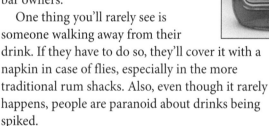

One thing you'll rarely see is someone walking away from their drink. If they have to do so, they'll cover it with a napkin in case of flies, especially in the more traditional rum shacks. Also, even though it rarely happens, people are paranoid about drinks being spiked.

There are locally produced wines, but these are really only good for cooking. Plenty of good-quality wines are available, imported by and available from the larger supermarkets around the island.

The most popular wines are of the roots and tonic variety. The Jamaican market is nearly saturated with products designed to aid energy or sexual performance. Red Label and Magnum are fortified wines. Also popular are drinks like Jagra and Power Wine, containing Horny Goat Weed, a powerful aphrodisiac better known as Epimedium, or Yin

Yang Huo in Chinese medicine. Older brands, such as Wincarnis, Stone's, and Sanatogen, are also drunk.

There are some very fine dark rums available, but be wary of the white rums, especially a locally produced illegal moonshine known as John Crow Batty (a John Crow is a name for the commonly seen vultures that circle the skies over the island, and batty is short for backside—so, "vulture's bottom").

John Crow—What's In a Name?

Some believe the Jamaican bird also known as the carrion crow, or turkey vulture, was named after an Irish clergyman, the Reverend John Crow, who lived in Port Royal in the 1680s. It's claimed that he preached a sermon saying that transported prisoners should yield to the authorities. The bird's appearance reminded his audience of the unpopular priest, so they gave it his name in derision. Most researchers don't believe in that theory.

Another popular view is that the name may be linked to Jim Crow and the racial segregation laws in the USA.

The name has also gone into some common sayings:

"Every John Crow tink him pickney white." (Everyone thinks his own kid is the best.)

"If yuh fly wid John Crow yuh wi nyam dead meat." (A person who keeps bad company can be made to do bad things.)

Jamaica has a long tradition of brewing beer, and has a couple of fine examples, but over recent years younger drinkers have been increasingly buying import lager—worrying for the companies who made their names as Jamaica's favorites.

THE BEACH

The beach is a popular place to hang out on weekends if it is close by. There are usually plenty of food stalls at the more frequented destinations, serving fresh, locally caught seafood in a variety of styles from stamp and go—a fried fish fritter—to lobster. To drink there will be coconut water, ginger beer, or Ting—a refreshing, locally made, grapefruit drink. If there isn't a bar playing music, someone will get a car close enough for you to feel the bass.

You'll see people in groups, exercising, swimming, and generally playing around in the water. Many are not strong swimmers, but they take to the sea with gusto, often wearing clothes that aren't swimwear, especially the more mature members of the party. Adults will generally leave visitors alone, but children will often approach people who look different, and may want to play—or simply stare.

WHAT TO WEAR

Jamaica is very conservative in many ways, and if you're attending a business event it's advisable to keep it smart. People who can afford to dress well do so, and class and socioeconomic background go a long way in Jamaican society. In other situations it will be clear that Jamaica's fashion sense is diverse, to say the least: the styles you'll see at a downtown street party are far from acceptable only a few miles up the road at some of the bars and clubs in uptown Kingston, but one thing remains constant—they've made an effort. People really do believe you are what you wear. Folks who can sometimes barely afford enough to survive will hit the road looking so smart that it can embarrass a visitor who is not used to this. Sometimes, though, it may be advisable to dress down to avoid drawing attention to oneself, especially in areas that could be rough.

Only a few places ask for formal wear, but walking into some restaurants in the bigger tourist areas in beachwear may elicit frowns.

TIPPING

The proximity of the USA, where the majority of visitors come from, has led to tipping becoming common practice in the tourist areas. In hotels, from check-in staff to the porter to the man who'll "look after your car," a tip is expected, The burden of lugging your bags also requires a tip of perhaps US $1 or 2 a bag.

Most Jamaicans don't tip in a bar, but a visitor is expected to tip between J$.50 and 1.00 a drink. In a restaurant it's 15 percent of the total. Make sure you put the tip into the hand of your server—don't leave it on the table and walk away. In the average rum shack it's a courteous gesture to give "a little something."

With taxis in Kingston and route taxis all over the island, there's no need to tip, but JUTA and JCAL companies that are registered to carry tourists are more expensive, and their drivers do expect a tip.

On many excursions tipping is actually not allowed, but clever or daring staff will still try to find a way to get money out of the unsuspecting visitor.

Generally, however, don't tip where you don't get good service.

culture smart! jamaica

Winning Ways

I once asked a Jamaican who the best tourists were. The response wasn't about who were the most fun, or the friendliest, but came down to who tipped the most! The Americans were the best, followed by the Canadians, and the Europeans were the worst, especially the British. It may be something you aren't used to, but it's become part of the culture here.

GIVING "A SMALL CHANGE"

You may hear someone ask you for "a small change." The expected donation would normally be about J$100. The frequency that you'll be asked can sometimes be quite annoying, especially because in some cases what you give will be used to buy drugs. If you feel that an individual might become a nuisance, a polite "no, sorry" will be enough for them to move on.

TOWN SQUARES AND SHOPPING MALLS

Everything happens at the clock towers, squares, and plazas in the heart of the commercial district in all the towns. Hives of activity during the day, in the hours after 5:00 p.m. they are packed full of taxis jockeying to take passengers home as others get ready for a

night out. People try to buy and sell amid a cacophony of noise as sound systems boom out the biggest tunes of today and yesterday.

SPORTS AND EXERCISE

Physical activity is important to Jamaicans, who aim for the body beautiful. The accepted norms of beauty in Jamaica, however, are different from those in the USA and Europe. Having a "Coca-Cola bottle shape" is closer to the ideal for women—Jamaicans like a more voluptuous figure and appreciate curves. It's also linked to money—plumpness is a sign of good health, good nourishment, and fertility. Being thin, or *mauger* (Jamaican Patois for "meager") is not considered attractive in Jamaica, and thin women will often be encouraged to eat more. When people put on weight strangers will tell them so, much to the horror of foreigners who have gained a few

pounds on vacation! Locals will say how well they look now that they are fatter. Jamaicans may now be more accepting of different body shapes and sizes, but people do enjoy eating and living well if they can afford it.

Every morning before the sun comes up you'll see Jamaicans of all ages exercising, particularly running or walking along the sides of the roads, and in the heat of the day you'll see many people on bikes, especially in Kingston, where cycling is more popular, and also on tennis courts around the country. The tourist industry has led the country to produce a large number of good tennis coaches, who in many cases end up being employed abroad.

The island is the biggest market in the world, per head of population, for cranberry juice and other cranberry products. A high prostate cancer rate combined with canny marketing means that anything that contains the super fruit sells.

Athletics

Jamaica's love of athletics is well-known, and their prowess in the field is a symbol of national pride. The country is now a superpower in sprinting, with its athletes picking up a large number of medals in international competitions. This is in part due to a coaching program that was started in the 1970s in collaboration with the Cuban government. The plan was to see each school have a dedicated coach. Another reason for the island's sporting success is due to the National Boys' and Girls' Championships. For the past century the four-day event sees schools from across the country battle it out for the title of King and Queen of the competition. Around 30,000 spectators attend what is in essence a glorified sports day, but in Jamaica the event has nationwide coverage on TV, on radio, and in the newspapers, and has given some of Jamaica's finest athletes their first taste of success. Over the weekend the National Stadium is full of past and present pupils cheering on their old schools.

Cricket

For over a century cricket was the main game of Jamaica, and in many ways it was more than a game. A great sense of national pride came from the clash against England, the colonial power. You'll still see people at local matches, and when there is an international test you'll be pressed to find anything else on television, but matches aren't well attended locally because of the cost. The corporate boxes, however, are crammed as a Who's Who of Jamaican businesses wines and dines its clients.

Soccer

Much of the decline of cricket is due to the growing popularity of football. The sport is now the dominant game on the island, with matches taking place at the start of the day and in the early evening. You'll see cars lined up by the side of the road anywhere there's a patch of open grass. The popularity of the game as a spectator sport can be seen during the football season, where most young men will go to matches in the local Jamaican premier league and also support teams in the English leagues.

CULTURAL LIFE

The Jamaican Cultural Development Commission puts on art exhibitions, training, and festivities leading up to the yearly Independence Day celebrations in August. It also holds a song competition, running since 1966, that has been a stepping-stone into the mainstream for many Jamaican artists who are now internationally known, like Toots and the Maytals, and Desmond Dekker. High culture remains the preserve of the uptown society set, and there is little ripple effect to the working classes.

Art

The first recorded graphic art in Jamaica came from its early inhabitants. The indigenous Taino left behind rock carvings, known as petroglyphs, and pottery. Very few examples of the cave art (pictograms) still exist, but this pre-Columbian work was the start of a long tradition.

The country's art scene grew during the colonial era. The style was initially based on figurative depictions of the landscape of the New World created by traveling artists making a living by painting for aristocrats in Europe. The most famous native-born artist was Isaac Mendes Belisario (1795–1849), who took a more Jamaica-centric approach to the island. His paintings and lithographs provide a fascinating insight into the lives of the Africans and landowners in post-emancipation Jamaica.

In the modern era, Edna Manley's arrival on the scene in 1922 was the beginning of a new style of art in Jamaica. Married to the future Prime Minister, Norman Manley, she challenged the Europeanized view of art on the island that, like the society of the time, looked toward the

motherland and didn't reflect the
Jamaica she loved. She wanted to let
artists be themselves and create from the
traditions that had survived from
Africa. Her legacy is still felt. The
Jamaica School of Art was
renamed the Edna Manley
College of the Visual Arts, as a
tribute to the work she did in
promoting the arts in Jamaica.

Much of Jamaica's art is now
split between more traditional self-taught artists
rooted in African expression known as the
"Intuitives" and the trained artists known as
"Mainstream" who use trends from abroad as part
of their style.

Dance

In 1790 the slave owner William Beckford wrote,
in *A Descriptive Account of the Island of Jamaica*,
"Not withstanding all their hardships, they are
fond of play and merriment; and if not prevented
by whites, by the law of the island, they will meet
on Saturday nights, hundreds of them in gangs,
and dance and sing till morning, nay sometimes
they continue their balls without intermission till
Monday morning."

The same is pretty much still true. Turn on
the TV, and you'll see dancing on the local
stations, on music videos, or on the popular
Dancing Dynamites, a talent show judged by
some of the island's top choreographers. This style

of dance came out of dancehall culture; the music's popularity has spawned dance nights in Kingston where patrons can dance virtually 24/7, on Good Sunday, Hot Monday, Early Tuesday, Weddy Weddy, Jiggy Friday.

Contemporary dance is also popular. Rooted in African traditional and folk dance, it has now fused elements of dancehall into its repertoire. Every year new dance moves become popular to go with a new song, but they all trace their development from early African dances such as the Calimbe, the Dinki Mini, and Gerreh, and European forms such as maypole dancing and quadrilles that were danced by the island's enslaved peoples.

Literature

Jamaican literature has been influenced by the many nations that made the island their own, but the predominant force has again been that of African Jamaicans. The oral tradition of West Africa was passed on from generation to generation and created Anancy stories—Ashanti folk tales of a spider-man who used his guile, quick-wittedness, and intelligence to survive. His stories, told to Jamaican children as bedtime stories, have survived the horrors of slavery to this day. Parents still tell the tales now, either from memory or from books, but traditionally in rural communities the matriarchs would pass them on, surrounded by the children—a treat that would go on into the night. These stories of triumph over adversity were invaluable in a black society that was dominated by a white minority during slavery. Anancy used his cunning and guile to survive—a similar trait that the enslaved needed to make good of their situation.

Riddles and proverbs were also popular forms, but that all changed in the 1940s and '50s, at the start of a new wave of writing from the West Indies. The BBC World Service began broadcasting the programs "Caribbean Voices" and "Calling the West Indies" that gave international writers such as Derek Walcott and V. S. Naipaul, and Jamaican poet Louise Bennett, their first exposure to a wider audience. The island continues to produce some of the best writers in the region and is now home to the largest literary festival in the Caribbean—the Calabash International Literary Festival, which takes place annually at Treasure Beach in St. Elizabeth. Held at Jake's Resort, a boutique hotel on the south coast, it hosts workshops, storytelling, poetry, music, and readings from some of the most established and up-and-coming writers from around the globe.

NIGHTLIFE

Jamaica has a vibrant nightlife. However, the nation's battle with violent crime can make the choices narrower for tourists than they should be. On weekends there are always "stageshows" (reggae and dancehall concerts) and "dances" (sound-system parties). Most people love to dance, and there is great pride in the semi-choreographed moves that you'll see at street dances and round robin events around the island. The main hot spots for the club scene are Kingston, Montego Bay, Negril, and Ocho Rios. The capital has some of the best: there's The Office and, the two most established venues, Quad, run by Brian "Ribbie" Chung, and The Asylum, now used for special events only. Pure/Plush Night Club and Lounge and Fiction are two newcomers on the scene that are becoming the favored hangouts to see and be seen. In Montego Bay, Pier One is popular with locals, while Margaritaville gathers a mixed clientele with lots of tourists, and Blue Beat is aimed at the expat and well-heeled Montegonian crowd. In Ocho Rios, Amnesia, The Roof, and the town's branch of Margaritaville are the top picks.

If you're looking for variety there isn't much, with reggae and dancehall being mainly what you'll hear, but don't be too surprised if the selector (DJ) throws on some disco or even country and western. At stageshows the island's top artists will perform at open-air venues. Sumfest, held every July in Montego Bay, is one of the biggest annual events; it has more of an international feel, and is aimed at tourists as well as locals. The roots reggae of Western Consciousness in Savanna La Mar and Rebel Salute in St. Elizabeth give way to the more hardcore dancehall of Sting in Portmore—these are solidly local affairs, and cater to true fans of the music. The Jazz Festival held in Montego Bay is also a popular event, with a large international lineup. Such occasions are generally peaceful and trouble free.

Music

Jamaica's musical heritage is very rich. From Rastafari drumming to reggae, mento, and ska, the island's heritage goes far beyond its most famous son, Bob Marley. The other island sounds, such as

calypso and soca, have also contributed to the island's musical development, but reggae and dancehall are the two styles you'll hear virtually everywhere. If you're sensitive to noise, Jamaica isn't the place for you. The island has a soundtrack: everywhere you go you'll hear music. Elsewhere it would be termed noise pollution, here it's just the way it is. You'll hear it blasting from taxis and homes, from outside and inside shops, from vendors in pushcarts, and through the speakers at the National Stadium. And the country's religious traditions that see almost everyone attend church as a child ensure that gospel music, especially the compositions of the American Baptists and Pentecostals, still plays a major role in the sounds of the island.

Mento

Having started at the end of the nineteenth century, mento, based on Jamaican folk music, sounds similar to calypso from Trinidad. It rose to international prominence just as it was dying in popularity on the island. The 1950s saw the start of the local recording industry as Stanley Motta taped artists, but the arrival of the electricity grid saw more and more musicians move away from its acoustic sound as mobile sound systems became popular. Mento remained a staple with tourists, and mento bands are now most commonly heard at resorts, although veteran artists such as the Jolly Boys are now appealing to a new international audience.

R&B

American R&B on the sound systems was the new sound of Jamaica in the 1950s, as stations transmitting out of Florida created a new taste and scene. Prince Buster, Duke Reid, and Clement "Coxsone" Dodd were the biggest selectors (DJs), importing the latest US sounds to a hungry Jamaican audience, but when there was a lack of new material they began recording local acts to satisfy the demands of the public for fresh music.

Ska

As the popularity of R&B waned, ska arose in the late 1950s. The guitar- and trumpet-led sound was initially instrumental, but soon popular singers such as Desmond Dekker, Toots Hibbert, and Bob

Marley became stars singing in this style. In 1964 Millie Small's "My Boy Lollipop" became an international hit in both the USA and the UK. The record was produced by Chris Blackwell, who went on to become a legend in the recording industry.

Ska's popularity grew alongside that of Rastafari, with song lyrics taking on Rastafarian themes; slower beats and chants entered the music, and ska soon evolved into rocksteady.

Rocksteady
Alton Ellis is said to have coined the term "rocksteady." His track "Get Ready Rock Steady" was a new dance that started a new phase in Jamaican music. It was the sound of Jamaica's "rude boys." They were from the poor, inner-city communities of Kingston, but they dressed in the latest styles on the street and in the dancehalls. Wearing porkpie and trilby hats, matched with sharp suits and thin ties, they expressed the dissatisfaction of a generation of youth that felt that they had missed the boat in postcolonial Jamaica. The music has heavy emphasis on the bass line, as opposed to ska's strong horn section, and the rhythm guitar began playing on the upbeat and become the foundation of modern reggae and dancehall.

Reggae
By the early 1970s, rocksteady had evolved into reggae, which combines elements from American soul music with the traditional shuffle and one-drop of Jamaican mento. Reggae quickly became

popular around the world, due in large part to the international success of artists like Bob Marley, Peter Tosh, and Bunny Wailer. Marley was viewed as a Rastafarian messianic figure by

some fans, particularly throughout the Caribbean, Africa, and among Native Americans and Australian Aborigines. His lyrics about love, redemption, and natural beauty captivated audiences, and he gained headlines for negotiating truces between the two opposing Jamaican political parties (at the One Love Concert), led by Michael Manley (PNP) and Edward Seaga (JLP). Reggae music was intricately tied to the expansion of the Rastafarian religion, and its principles of pacifism and pan-Africanism. Musicians like Gregory Isaacs, The Congos, and Burning Spear, and producers like Lee "Scratch" Perry solidified the early sound of reggae.

Theater and Cinema
Most of the major cities—Montego Bay, Mandeville, Ocho Rios, and Kingston—have multiplexes. However, the cost of tickets has seen an explosion in bootleg DVDs for sale on the streets. The quality is very low, but it has become a real issue for the authorities on the island. The problem is made worse for Jamaican cinema. The

popularity of local productions, such as *Third World Cop* or *Dancehall Queen*, is so high that many don't make much money because of widespread illegal copying in Jamaica and then in the diaspora.

Theater, particularly comedy, farce, and satire, is hugely popular in Jamaica. Ads are carried on TV with the funniest lines from the script used as a trailer for the production. The plays are written in patois that visitors may struggle to understand. The atmosphere at performances is that of unbridled fun, as they are quite bawdy and have lots of sexual innuendo. Audience participation is high, especially when the shows hit the road. They start their runs in Kingston but then tour the provincial towns, often playing in unconventional venues such as school halls. They, too, eventually get transferred to video, and again suffer from widespread bootlegging. The Barn, The Centre Stage, The Little Theatre, The Pantry, New Kingston Theatre, and the Phillip Sherlock Centre for the Creative Arts are the main venues in the capital.

PLACES TO VISIT
Dunns River Falls

Located near Ocho Rios, the Dunns River Falls are the island's chief attraction. More than a million visitors a year see these famous waterfalls. The cascades run from a height of around 600 feet
(183 m) over a series of rocks and boulders down to a sandy beach. Climbing the falls is a must-do—note that water shoes are needed to scramble up to the

top. Local guides are so used to the terrain that they run up, while visitors hold hands to make the ascent. The site is overdeveloped, but is still very pretty. Jamaican residents pay less than tourists, so there is always a healthy mix inside the state-run property.

Nine Miles
The island's most famous son, the reggae singer Bob Marley, was born in Nine Miles, the small village in St. Ann that now houses his mausoleum. The links to the star are still strong in the area. A school started by his wife, Rita, is close by, and occasionally his family can be found there. All the guides on-site are local, and some knew Marley himself when he was alive. It's very touristy, with children singing Bob Marley songs and higglers trying to sell everything from candy to ganja. The smoking of marijuana is tolerated on the site, but it is still illegal. Every year thousands of people gather at Nine Miles to celebrate the singer's birth and death.

Green Grotto Caves

This site, on the island's North Coast between Runaway Bay and Discovery Bay, was used by the Taino Indians for rituals in pre-Columbian days, and was also a burial place for the tribe. During the last days of the Spanish occupation of the island the Spanish hid boats in the caves in order to escape from the English and flee to Cuba, and slaves also hid there when they ran away from the plantations. The caves are interconnected and easily accessible, and lead down to a great subterranean lake. As you look up in the large cavern you can see tree roots from above snaking down through the rock toward the water.

Blue Lagoon

This spectacular deep lagoon, which changes color according to the time of day, is near Port Antonio, in Portland. Some people claim that is a bottomless hole, but it is actually 170.6 feet (52 m) deep, and opens up to the sea via a narrow funnel. It is fed by freshwater springs. The movie *Blue Lagoon*, starring Brooke Shields, was filmed here in the 1980s. Access used to be easy, through a restaurant overlooking the hole, but destruction by a series of hurricanes saw its closure. You can still get to the public area, however, with locals who sail round.

Frenchman's Cove

Frenchman's Cove, also near Port Antonio, is a hotel with a private beach that the public can access on payment of a small entrance fee. It is a breathtakingly beautiful cove, with a stream flowing into the sea, where time seemingly stops. There is a small restaurant, serving Jamaican dishes, and a bar with cold beer. This mainly attracts vacationers—but discerning ones, who are in the know.

Rio Grande

In Port Antonio you can ride down the river on bamboo rafts. These carry two people at a sedate pace down the slow-moving rapids with Jamaica's highest peaks, the Blue Mountains, as a background. This was how bananas were transported down from the plantations to the wharves during the 1900s for export to the USA and Europe.

In the 1930s Errol Flynn came to Jamaica and bought a home on the island. He decided that rafting would be a great way to idle the time away, and so started a tradition that exists to this day.

Rose Hall, Montego Bay

This plantation house on the outskirts of Kingston is renowned for the ghost of its former owner, Annie Palmer, who is said to haunt the property. She was born in Haiti, where they say she became a voodoo priestess. She moved to Jamaica to marry a wealthy landowner who died mysteriously, leaving her the 6,000-acre estate. Locals believe she killed three husbands and numerous slave lovers before one finally stabbed

her to death. She was given the name the White Witch, and her ghost is claimed to have been seen by a number of visitors.

The Marine Park, Montego Bay

This offers glass-bottomed boat tours to showcase the underwater life around the coast. Overfishing has somewhat depleted stocks around the island, but the guides can explain their role in the conservation and protection of the marine environment.

Falmouth

In nearby Falmouth, visitors can see another historic plantation house. Greenwood Great House is more than two hundred years old, and was owned by the family of English poets Robert Browning and Elizabeth Barrett-Browning. It is one of the best-preserved Great Houses of Jamaica.

Falmouth itself has one of the highest concentrations of Georgian architecture in the Caribbean. Many of them are in a dilapidated state but a new development, planned to include the restoration of the historic buildings and dredging of the waterfront, will see large cruise ships berthing in the town.

Falmouth's luminous lagoon is a natural wonder, in which unique microbial organisms in the water create phosphorescent light when disturbed. You can take a boat trip for a ride on the lagoon at dusk, and when you swim or even wave your hands in the water it glows in the dark.

Culture Yard, Kingston

This is the former home of Bob Marley. Those familiar with the reggae star's music will remember him singing about "a tenement yard in Trench Town." Well, this is the home he lived in with wife, Rita, at the start of his career. It is now run as a simple museum, and is a way to see parts of downtown Kingston that shaped a legend.

Bob Marley Museum, St. Andrew

This museum, devoted to the late reggae superstar, is housed in his former studio uptown. It had previously belonged to Chris Blackwell, his manager, and Bob Marley's moving to the area at the time caused some controversy. Now the colonial building is a National Heritage site, kept much the way it was at his death.

Devon House, St. Andrew

This house was built by George Steibel in 1881, the son of a Jewish merchant and a Jamaican housekeeper. Steibel became the island's first black millionaire by investing in Venezuelan gold mines. The law of the time restricted the amount

of landholdings a black man could own to one hundred, so he purchased ninety-nine properties on the island. Devon House was built on fifty-three acres of land in Kingston and designed in the "Jamaican-Georgian" style. The house is furnished with antiques from France, England, Jamaica, and the Caribbean.

On weekends you'll see a large cross-section of Kingstonians at Devon House, as I Scream, housed here, is one of the nation's favorite ice cream stores, and Norma's On The Terrace provides high-end dining.

Jamaica's National Gallery

This is a quiet diversion. Located not far from the harbor front in downtown Kingston, it contains the pick of the nation's art. Its collection ranges from the Intuitives—self-taught local artists who draw on a more Afrocentric tradition—to the work of early masters like Belisario, to modern works by Manley and Kapo, a revivalist minister who depicted themes of the faith.

Port Royal

Port Royal, not far from the airport, was a pirate den during the seventeenth century, and known as "the wickedest city on earth." Much of the old town sank under fifty feet of water after an earthquake in 1692. Many of the buildings from the colonial area remain, however, and Port Royal feels like a different world from Kingston, just across the water.

Negril

Everyone seemingly heads to the west end of Negril to look at the sunsets. This is the most westerly point of the island, and as the light fades the excitement begins. Rick's Café is the most famous spot, where patrons enjoy live music and one of the island's best views, and can watch local young men dive into the water from dizzying heights.

Black River

Jamaica's longest river meets the sea at the small town of Black River. It's a haven for crocodiles, and there are a number of tour companies that provide tourists with a chance to see them. The mangroves provide an ideal location to watch birds and relax on a journey upriver.

chapter seven

TRAVEL, HEALTH, & SAFETY

Travel around Jamaica is getting better, but it's still a test for the visitor. The geographical distance between Kingston and the second city, Montego Bay, is only 130 miles (209 km), but the journey takes three and a half or four hours because of the road conditions. There has been extensive road building over the last decade, and many of the routes to the main towns have been repaired or rebuilt.

A modern highway runs along much of the north coast, connecting the resorts, and sections of toll road have been built out of Kingston to Portmore. The plan is for this road network to run between the capital and Montego Bay and to take in parts of other parishes, including St. Catherine, Manchester, St. Elizabeth, Westmoreland, Hanover, and St. Ann. The new roads are understandably in excellent condition. However, there are still huge potholes in the towns and on the myriad roads leading to the small surrounding communities. Journey into any of the towns and you'll soon be confronted with roads that are in need of repair. White marl is often used to patch the road where water, especially during the hurricane season, has destroyed the surface. Because of the rain this hasty solution stays in place for months until it is eventually washed away. Drivers will do anything to avoid mishaps such as their cars bottoming out in holes, burst tires, bent rims, and their vehicles' suspension being "mashed up." Beware of drivers coming toward you on the other side of the road and swerving in front of you to avoid the bumps on their side.

ROUTE TAXIS
In Jamaica it's expensive to import motor vehicles— the cost of the duties levied is nearly the same as the cost of the vehicle. There's a large market for Toyotas, especially the cheaper models, which are shipped direct from Japan and not spray painted but left in the base white color. These are the most common vehicles on the road, and the Corolla the most popular model. The low cost, plus the availability of spares, makes them the choice of people who "run" taxis.

You can spot taxis by the red plates with the letters PP or PPV on the front of the vehicles; the names of the areas they cover are on the doors. They are known as "route taxis," because they go from one specific location to another. They are supposed to carry four passengers, but routinely they'll squeeze as many passengers into the back as they can. The bane of their lives is the Taxi Authority, which regulates drivers, and the police, who often ticket them for speeding. Drivers want to make as many trips as possible during the day, so speeding is common.

Route taxis run quite short distances but are incredible value for money in comparison to the tourist buses and minivans that operate out of the hotels. For between J$90 and 350 you can move between the main travel hubs. If you plan to travel across the country via route taxi it is possible to do so, but expect lots of stops.

You'll sometimes see a crowd of people crammed into a white car that looks like a taxi but does not have the red plates. These are unlicensed taxis, known as robots. Locals often use these rogue cabs, but you don't know whose car you're jumping into, so they are best avoided if they stop for you.

It is quite inexpensive to charter a route taxi for a day. Either call an established company or get a driver on the street you feel comfortable with. Expect to give a driver around US$150 a day, plus gas. It's essential to negotiate the fare before you set off. Many taxi drivers say "I'll give you a special price," and then at the end of the day they ask for much more than you'd expected.

"COASTERS"

Toyota minibuses, called coasters, ply their trade mainly between the main towns. They often have window tints, with designs on the front windshield and others on the sides. They don't leave at scheduled times but wait till the bus is full, so sitting on one while it fills up can be very tedious. It is quite possible, especially during the day, to wait for hours until enough people are on board. To make things worse people will get on, secure a seat, and then leave, creating the illusion that hardly anybody is going. While the ductor (conductor) tries to get everyone on board higglers will get on and offer you a wide range of goods, from donuts and sweet drinks to CDs, DVDs, and phone cards. The transportation center itself nearly always has cooked food for sale. Toilet attendants charge around J$20 for use of the conveniences.

On board, you'll be as squashed as you'd be in a route taxi. There's always a sign indicating how many "persons" the vehicle is licensed to carry, but that is often ignored. Drivers squeeze an extra person into each row, and this leads to protests if the extra person is rather large! People may refuse to allow them to take a seat, and this sometimes results in a complete rearrangement of the seating. There are some padded wooden seats, which fold down and straddle the gangway that people need to move to the exit, which means that if someone at the back of the bus wants to get off a lot of people have to stand up to let them pass.

You'll often see a bus loaded up with goods for sale at the market, especially in the mornings, when the higglers will take an extra seat for their packages. Most of these medium-sized buses have no extra space for baggage, which has to go between your feet or on your lap, only adding to the discomfort.

Despite this, there's a real sense of camaraderie and humor on the buses. Sometimes arguments break out that will involve the entire bus, or a sermon played on CD will get people agreeing with the pastor. Dancehall can be pumping from the locally made speakers that would put a sound system to shame, and the speeds can be breakneck, but after the journey, as the driver or ductor collects the fares, you know you've experienced something uniquely Jamaican.

The macho attitude toward driving means that everyone believes they were born with top-ranking

racing skills. Any kind of maneuver on the part of a driver, especially parking, will see lots of people offering help and advice— most of it unneeded and unwanted.

DRIVING

Driving is notoriously bad in Jamaica. The road death toll is around three hundred a year, and the country spends about five million US dollars a year in treating the thousands who are injured. Many drivers drive at speeds unsuitable for the conditions, or drive downright recklessly. You'll see people pulling out from intersections as another vehicle is speeding toward them, forcing both to stop, and you'll see drivers, bored with waiting in a line of traffic, pull out to pass the stationary traffic, on the wrong side of the road, with vehicles coming headlong toward them. Cars often speed up when approaching crossing pedestrians, and slow down in the fast lane when other vehicles want to pass them. Other drivers are overly polite, and their behavior can also cause accidents, for example by stopping to allow pedestrians to cross the road at a dangerous place, either causing a collision behind them, or causing other drivers to pass them and hit those crossing.

Drivers tend to drive using their horns to alert others to their presence, and they also use hand signals—such as a hand waved up and down to indicate to those behind to slow down.

For most drivers in Jamaica the best defense when driving is offense. As a visitor, the best approach to take is to drive with extra care. Virtually everyone apart from beginners and the near infirm drive aggressively, and you'll need to be constantly aware when using the country's roads, both as a driver and as a pedestrian.

Rules of the Road

As a former British colony, Jamaica follows similar road rules, and driving is on the left. One of the main differences, however, is the use of the horn—to warn other drivers not to carry out moves that will impede your progress, or not to make dangerous maneuvers, and to alert others to your presence.

Standard international road signs are used across the island, although in rural communities these are often missing.

The driver and front-seat passengers must wear seat belts. Most people don't, however, unless they see members of the Island Special Constabulary. These are the police officers with the blue seams on their trousers, whose primary job is to enforce the country's road traffic act. The responsibility is yours to "buckle up" and if as a passenger you don't, you, rather than the driver, will face the fine.

The speed limit is 70 mph (112 kph) on the highways and 30 mph (48 kph) on other roads. Many drivers go above these speeds, and police speed traps are in operation across the island. Speeding tickets require a court appearance. The cost will be around J$5,000.

Some police officers use their authority to impose fines for traffic violations as a way of boosting their income, and bribery isn't uncommon. The Jamaica Constabulary Force and the Island Special Constabulary Force are attempting to stamp out corruption with sting operations. However, if you are stopped don't instigate any kind of bribe, as you could end up facing a much bigger charge than for a minor driving offense.

Sometimes it feels as if the festive season lasts all year in Jamaica, but drunk driving is in some ways less of an issue here than you might think. The inconvenience and the potential danger of traveling by public transportation at night means that many people who have cars might drive, but Jamaicans don't really condone those who drive when "under a few rum." This means that people will generally have a few drinks and head home rather than get drunk. The legal blood alcohol level is 0.08—the same as the USA, the UK, and Canada. The police regularly stop drivers and have recently implemented breathalyzer tests. If you fail this, four penalty points will be logged on your driving record, and if convicted you will be suspended from driving for a year.

However, one of the biggest problems on Jamaican roads is corruption of another sort. Many of the driver's licenses that have been issued have been bought, which means that many people behind the wheels have not been through any formal training.

If you are involved in an accident, call the police. Often minor accidents won't see a response, but stress to the authorities that you are a foreigner and they'll be there a lot sooner than if you were a local person making the call. However, this advice goes out the window if, in the worst scenario, you unfortunately hit a child. Offer to take the child to a hospital, and call the police, but if they don't appear quickly and things start looking ugly it may be best to lock the car doors and try to drive to the nearest police station. In such a situation Jamaican mob mentality and street justice can sometimes quickly cause things to get out of hand.

PEDAL POWER

In the more rural districts you'll see plenty of people walking, but fewer in the towns. More common are bicycles. "Rambos" is the name given locally to mountain bikes, and you'll see grown men riding around on children's bikes and kids on full-size adult frames. They are ridden for short trips around the streets in Kingston, used as communal property among friends, and are a modern beast of burden in the country, where you can see even long branches of bamboo transported by bike, little red rags attached to the ends to signify the long load.

TRAINS

Jamaica has one of the oldest railways in the western hemisphere, but the network, which also saw one of the biggest train crashes in history at Kendall in the 1950s, hasn't been run for passengers for well over a quarter of a century. The only things transported on the remaining infrastructure are bauxite and alumina, and parts of the old line have now been "captured" by squatters. However, there are plans to reintroduce a freight and passenger network, and a deal with the Chinese to reopen sixteen new stations across the island. This will ease congestion on the roads, especially in the urban centers.

PLANES

Flying is an expensive but very quick option for getting around the island. Private helicopters are the preserve of the rich and famous, or of tourists with money to spare who want a fast transfer to their hotels from the airport. The scheduled flights on medium-sized propeller planes are normally full of businessmen and -women going between Kingston, known locally as "town," and "Mobay," or Montego Bay. For most destinations it's a short trip—it feels as if you are preparing to land almost as soon as you take off. The intra-island airports are Ken Jones in Portland, Tinson Pen in Kingston, Sangster International in Montego Bay, Negril airfield in Westmoreland, and Boscobel in St. Mary, which also serves Ocho Rios. This last airfield is under expansion to allow larger jets to land in the northwest. Portland has been designated as the location for Jamaica's high-end tourist market, and they see Boscobel as the gateway for that part of the country.

There is now a small company offering daily flights between Montego Bay and Kingston. For most of the internal airports you'll fly in a single-engine Cessna, but an alternative is to fly by helicopter—at a price, of course. There are also plans for a seaplane service between Montego Bay in the northwest and parts of the south coast.

WHERE TO STAY

To suit the vacationers who flock here year after year, Jamaica has plenty of rooms in a wide variety of properties, from luxury five-star hotels to private villas and bed and breakfasts. The most popular places tend to be the north-coast resort towns of

Ocho Rios, Montego Bay, and Negril in the west, but other more rural spots like San Antonio in Portland in the northeast and Treasure Beach on the south coast are good options.

Many people avoid Kingston because of its reputation for crime, but this is a pity when it has so

much to offer. Its nightlife is superior to that of anywhere else. The music that the island is known for came out of the bustling inner city, and "town," as Jamaicans call it, is the heart of the island. To understand the country you need to see what makes it tick. Kingston is faster paced than nearly anywhere else in the Caribbean—but this will also make you appreciate the old-time rural Jamaica that can still be found in villages in the interior, especially in Cockpit Country, in Trelawney, renowned for its yams and its most famous son, Usain Bolt.

HEALTH

There are hospitals in all the fourteen parishes, but those in Kingston and Montego Bay are better equipped and offer full emergency treatment. Government-run ambulances with paramedics operate only in parts of the island—the northwest of the country from Falmouth in Trelawney through to Negril in Westmoreland, and in the south Linstead, in St. Catherine. They have specially trained firefighters, who also work as emergency medical technicians. In outlying parishes, and even in Kingston, there is no such coverage, and there are now a number of private operators who run services, but the quality of care can vary widely.

Most hotels either have an on-call medical service on-site, or they'll send guests to a private hospital for treatment. Doctors in these private facilities will require payment before treatment, and the final bill can run into the tens of thousands, so it is important to get adequate medical insurance that includes repatriation if needed. There are pharmacies in most towns that can dispense medication. Many of these, especially those in Kingston and Montego Bay, stay open late.

There are no specific vaccinations needed for travel to Jamaica, but it would be advisable to make sure you are immunized against hepatitis A and B; measles, mumps, and rubella; tetanus and diphtheria; and, if staying for extended periods in rural areas, typhoid.

The most common ailment to affect travelers is stomach upsets, generally caused by the change in food, water, and climate. Try to avoid eating food that has been left standing. Jamaicans generally don't undercook meat, but don't eat food that looks as if it is not properly cooked through, especially from fast-food outlets.

Drinking water in Jamaica is safe in the cities, but in the more rural areas, where water comes from drums, this is more suspect and bottled water should be drunk.

Sunburn

The tropical heat can burn exposed skin very quickly. High-factor sunscreen is needed; otherwise you will risk spending part of your holiday with skin that looks like third-degree burns and a tan that would put a lobster to shame. Even with heavy cloud cover you can ruin a vacation by underestimating the strength of the heat, especially in the summer months. If you do get burned, use peeled aloe vera leaf to soothe the pain.

Things that Bite and Sting

Wasps and bees often nest in roof spaces, so while admiring the view from a balcony you might get an unpleasant surprise from above. Red ants are easy to spot—they are big, bright red, and leave a nasty bite. "Forty legs" is the local name for a rather vicious centipede. "Sea eggs" is the Jamaican term for sea urchins; these spine-covered creatures make their homes in the rock pools on the shoreline. The common advice from Jamaicans is to pee on the injury after removing the spine from the flesh! The best thing about Jamaica in this regard is that there are no poisonous snakes.

There are, however, sand flies and mosquitoes aplenty. Mosquitoes are a painful nuisance here, but not a danger, though there have been reports of occasional cases of malaria in and around

Kingston. It is recommended that mosquito repellent be used to stop the insects biting, and sleeping under a mosquito net if your room doesn't have air-conditioning.

Sand flies, also known as "no see ums," are, as the name suggests, nearly invisible to the naked eye. Like mosquitoes, they make their presence felt toward nightfall. They seem to be resistant to nearly every kind of repellent, but they can't bite through clothing—unlike mosquitoes, who can bite through a tight-fitting garment.

The macka is a type of bush that has razor-sharp barbs, which, when fallen on the ground, can easily puncture the soles of light rubber footwear.

HIV

In this very sexually active country, HIV/AIDS has become a real issue, and official estimates put those said to be HIV positive at 1.5 percent of the population. Early sexual activity, multiple partners, older men sleeping with young girls, and boys needing to prove their manhood have brought about an epidemic here. The overall infection rate has declined, because older people have become more aware of the risks and there is wider use of contraception, but among younger people the infection rate is going up, with nearly 10 percent of newly reported cases in adolescents.

Discrimination against those with HIV is high, and many people would rather die an early death than know they are affected, or be spotted going into a clinic. If they were known to have the virus people would "scorn" them, refrain from touching them, and refuse food from them.

SAFETY

Crime is unfortunately a problem in Jamaica. People's lives are affected in the corporate areas or business centers of Kingston and St. Andrew, Spanish Town, Portmore, and other urban centers including its second city, the primary tourist destination of Montego Bay. The island is a transshipment point to the major drug markets— primarily of marijuana, and to a lesser extent cocaine. The dons are responsible for much of the trade, exploiting Jamaican links with the large diaspora communities in North America, Europe, and the UK, where there are sizeable markets for the drugs. Law enforcement agencies in these countries operate in Jamaica and work alongside the Jamaica Constabulary Force to try to stem the trade between the island and these nations.

For the average Jamaican, watching the local news makes depressing viewing. JLP and PNP governments since the 1970s have been trying to tackle violent crime with little success, and now the country has one of the highest murder rates in the world. However, foreigners rarely get attacked in Jamaica. The commonsense advice that is given in most places in the world applies: be aware of your surroundings and your possessions. In tourist destinations guys will approach you and offer to show you around for a small fee. Most are harmless, and can often give you an insight into their lives, but it can be a bit annoying to be approached for the umpteenth time by someone with a curious put-on North American accent who insists on showing you around!

For visitors to Jamaica crime is something they are unlikely to face. Criminals know that a crime perpetrated against a tourist will be investigated thoroughly and the international scrutiny means that the police will try to make a quick arrest. Because of this many will not target the tourists, despite the fact that they may carry more money for a two-week trip than many Jamaicans make in a year. Opportunist thefts do occur, and so in many of the popular resort areas you'll see pith-helmeted "tourist police." They are there to keep watch and to deter people from pestering vacationers.

In any emergency, your hotel and the regular police should be the first contact. Unless you can actually spot and identify the thief it is unlikely they'll be caught. Your details will be taken, and a description if you can give one, but with so many other crimes to deal with it is unlikely you'll get your things back. If there is a theft from your hotel room, however, the importance of the establishment's reputation means that a greater effort will be made to recover the stolen items.

chapter eight

BUSINESS BRIEFING

THE ECONOMIC CLIMATE

Jamaica is in dire need of major foreign investment, and has one of the slowest national growth rates in the western hemisphere. It has a predominantly import-based economy with very few exports. Progress has been lethargic, to say the least, and single-digit growth has left Jamaica at a disadvantage next to its regional competitors of Barbados, Trinidad, and the Dominican Republic.

The country's original cash crops of sugar, bananas, and cocoa have nearly disappeared. The bauxite and alumina production industry that was an essential contribution to the nation's foreign exchange reserves declined in the global economic crisis of 2008–9. Tourism has long been a key driver of the economy, and the country has been actively courting foreign investment in this area. A large number of Spanish vacation companies are opening properties on the island. The government wants to encourage more visitors from further afield than its traditional markets of North America and Western Europe.

Jamaica has great economic potential. Despite the problems of the past, it has a strong history of political stability, which, combined with capital market development, modern accountancy practices, and judicial quality, make it much stronger than many of its neighbors. The fact that it is the third-largest English-speaking nation in the western hemisphere also makes it an attractive option.

Lying so close to some of the world's busiest shipping lanes gives Jamaica a strong advantage. The port of Kingston is only thirty-two miles from the north–south and east–west trade routes and at the center of the region. It is now a major hub for international shipping close to the largest market for consumer goods in the world, the USA.

It has the world's seventh-largest natural harbor and boasts a modern port that is one of the busiest in the region. It is underutilized and, in recent years, a number of the major shipping lines have pulled out of the port, but there are plans to get them back.

Jamaica has from its earliest history been an exporter of raw materials (sugar, cocoa, bananas), but now its economy is based firmly on services, which account for 70 percent of the island's trade. The country's largest trading partners include the USA, the UK, Canada, France, Spain, Norway, Venezuela, the Netherlands Antilles, and other CARICOM (Caribbean Community and Common

Market) countries. They invest in a range of sectors including utilities, such as energy, financial services, mining, infrastructure, IT, and communications, as well as in tourism.

The government is also looking to invite foreign investment in other areas such as agriculture, the creative industries, and manufacturing. The country is a good investment prospect, but it needs to improve productivity, especially if it plans to compete regionally and internationally. Over the past decade workers in Jamaica have recorded an annual decline in earnings, but elsewhere in the Caribbean and Latin America growth has increased.

International and regional competition and the global economic crisis have added to the island's problems, and, combined with the double whammy of crime and corruption, are also hampering investment. The bill for security adds to the operational costs of many businesses as they try to stop theft and fraud. The World Bank reported that if Jamaica could cut its crime levels, especially its murder rate, to match that of Costa Rica, it would see growth of over 5 percent per year, as opposed to just over 1 percent on average seen over the past decade.

JAMAICAN BUSINESSES

Everywhere you look in Jamaica you'll see small businesses operating as people try to hustle. This small-scale entrepreneurship has led to a large gray economy, which some estimate at around 55 percent of all trade. There are a large number of family-owned businesses on the island, some of which are sole traders, some partnerships, and some small wholesale or retail operations. Others are large service-based multinationals. The Sandals resort chain is the best example of the latter, but in manufacturing names such as Matalon, Levy, and Appleton Rum are notable family firms.

The larger companies have a global perspective that makes them more open to discussion and reaching a decision is more of a shared exercise. Smaller firms, however, are still very much boss-driven and hierarchical. Some of the bigger family firms were formed during the slavery era and are still run by the descendants of the plantation owners. This has created in many workers a "top-down" view of their role within the company, with the result that they are not used to taking initiatives, as happens in more developed nations. You'll still hear people referring to someone in authority, or someone who deserves respect, as "bossman" or "bosswoman." This tradition of deference makes some workers believe that it's not their role to think outside the box; they expect to be given orders.

THE WORKFORCE

The island has a skilled, educated, English-speaking workforce, and several universities, but things are far from easy for those seeking work. The functional literacy of many school graduates needs to be improved. The country suffers from large numbers of unemployed and underemployed people. The latest statistics (2010) put the unemployment rate at 14.5 percent.

Jamaica has some of the oldest trade unions in the region. They were both popular and strong in the past, but the harsh economic climate over the past twenty years has eroded much of their power. The first labor organizations on the island date back to the late nineteenth century, but it wasn't until the 1930s and the foundation of the Bustamante Industrial Trade Union that the political importance of unionization was felt. The two biggest unions, the BITU and the National Workers Union, are both general unions linked to the two main political parties. There are still more than seventy unions on the island, covering a variety of specific industries in both public and private sectors.

Non-Jamaicans seeking employment on the island are required to get a work permit, which lasts between six months and a year.

GOVERNMENT AND BUSINESS

Depending on whom you ask, you will hear that the government is either very pro or very anti business. The ruling Jamaica Labour Party would say that they are on the side of the private sector, more right-leaning than the People's National

Party. Jamaica, like many former colonies, struggles with archaic structures in public regulatory bodies. You can often find yourself going from building to building and department to department looking for information and trying to get forms filled out. There are plans for more standardization and one-stop shops for commerce, but these have yet to become a reality.

In many respects, much more has been done to encourage foreign investment than local investment, but there is a growing push within the country to generate profits from value-added production. Instead of exporting raw materials, it is hoped to build foreign markets for finished products, such as coffee, which in the past was exported only as beans, and the finished products—and much greater value—were created abroad.

The Jamaican government faces one of the highest debt burdens in the world. Every person on the island owes nearly US$4,500 in loan repayments as soon as they are born. Much of the country's earnings, which should go into social programs and infrastructure, goes into paying back the cash that has been used by successive administrations to keep the economy afloat. The government promotes foreign investment in the  areas of biotechnology, aquaculture, nutraceutical production, ornamental horticulture, and agriculture. It offers incentives such as help in sending money back to the country of origin, tax holidays, and duty-free import of machinery and raw materials for certain businesses. Areas that earn or save foreign exchange, that generate employment, and that use local raw materials are also encouraged.

Taxation

Tax avoidance is a big issue for the Jamaican government. Noncompliance occurs across the board, from the higglers in the street to the professionals. A recent survey in the country recently found that out of five hundred doctors only one hundred were paying tax. Official figures show that only around 45 percent of businesses are compliant, including quite large companies. The government is actively trying to target individuals by offering tax amnesties and confiscating property.

THE BUSINESS RELATIONSHIP

In Jamaica the strength of business relationships is crucial. The best way to get things moving is to network and build relationships through a number of the organizations that exist on the island. A good connection through them will save a lot of time, effort, and money. If you know the right people, it is possible to sidestep the normal bureaucratic delays that can take months to deal with.

The Private Sector Organisation of Jamaica (PSOJ) was founded in the 1980s as a pressure group for bigger businesses on the island. It has since become the chief grouping of the main owners of capital. The connections within the organization are with the captains of industry, and their influence can be felt from the commercial district downtown to parliament. The same can be said of the Jamaica Manufacturers Association (JMA) and the Jamaica Chamber of Commerce, where a buddy system exists, and the contacts here can be essential for success.

Jamaican businesspeople are straight-talking and "no-nonsense," and they will appreciate the same approach in return. They are known within the region for their candor. As one businessman remarked, "Trinidadians have the gift of the gab, but Jamaicans cut straight to the chase."

The conservative nature of Jamaican society means that talking a good game will not give you any form of advantage. You have to deliver, and any lack of competence or substance will soon be apparent. In Jamaica, a "ginal" is a person who tries to con or mislead others for financial benefit. Mistrust of such individuals has made those in business wary of empty promises.

CORRUPTION

The country, like many in the region, has an issue with what Jamaicans call "bandulu"—from things falling off the back of a truck to alleged corruption involving government contracts or deals by political leaders. This, alongside political and familial nepotism, has had a debilitating effect on Jamaican business, sometimes resulting in people without the skills being put into positions of leadership. The problem also exists in the busy financial area downtown, from the markets to the stores, where business owners pay protection money to the criminal bosses, the "dons." The government is taking steps to stop extortion by trying to get people to come forward and participate in sting operations.

BUSINESS GIFTS

In business, small gifts are acceptable. A big or expensive gift would probably embarrass the recipient, as it would be perceived as trying to make them look small.

MEETINGS

The working day is from 9:00 or 10:00 a.m. until 5:00 or 6:00 p.m., with an hour for lunch. The best time to schedule meetings is probably between 10:00 a.m. and midday. The two main business centers are Kingston and Montego Bay.

Jamaican business meetings are slightly less stuffy than in Europe, and include some casual small talk or banter to build the relationship, but people will be quite direct and eager to get the deal moving. It's best to try to arrange a morning, as opposed to an afternoon, meeting, as minds will be more focused, especially if you aren't used to the heat of the country—the travel can be quite tiring even in air-conditioned vehicles.

For both sexes it's advisable to wear a suit, especially for first meetings. Once a relationship has been established it is also acceptable for men to wear smart trousers and a long-sleeved shirt. Women should always go for conservative business dress, as anything conceived as risqué can be damaging. It's a good idea to arrive at least fifteen minutes before any meeting—the night before, arrange with a taxi company to pick you up and ask them how long the journey should take at the time of day you need to travel. Then call back a few hours before on the day to confirm the pickup. It may take at least five minutes to get through security, which can be quite thorough and can make you late. As mentioned earlier, being late will be seen in a very bad light and will be considered disrespectful. Having said that, be prepared to wait yourself!

Jamaicans rarely use first names, and even introduce themselves by their surnames on first meeting. So avoid calling people by their first names until a good relationship has developed. The country is much more formal than the USA.

If you are making a presentation, go for a factual, bottom-line type of approach, perhaps with a dose of humor, especially if you can integrate some local knowledge. Try not to make it too long, and allow time for questions at the end of the session.

NEGOTIATIONS

The Jamaican negotiating style is straight to the bottom line. Negotiations may take place away from the office. Restaurants are a favorite location and, as you are a visitor, people will want to treat you to the undiscovered delights of a local restaurant well off the tourists' beaten path. In such a situation, offer to pay; this will set the right tone, but it is likely that your host will refuse.

Many a big deal has been clinched at the go-go clubs in Kingston and Montego Bay, or on fishing or bird shoots. The macho culture of Jamaican society makes these environments a good place to seal the deal and build the business relationship. Try not to drink too much, as many will see this as a sign that you're not a serious person and can't hold your liquor. It's worth bearing in mind that, regardless of the size of the business, you'll often be dealing with the decision makers right from the outset.

Once the deal is down on paper it is binding. The time for renegotiation is over once lawyers have written up the contract, which will be followed to the letter. Unless problems arise over fulfillment, there is no particular need to stay in touch personally. If there are delays, however, Jamaican businessmen won't appreciate playing phone tag to get hold of you, and the truth will be the best option.

MANAGING DISAGREEMENT

If there is a disagreement, getting in touch and not backing down, regardless of the anger or aggression you may face, is the best response. In this macho culture, those who seem to shy away from the confrontation may not be respected. People will take legal action if a contract isn't fulfilled, but will generally want to avoid going through the courts because of the expense of legal fees and the time taken for recourse. The courts are fair and effective, but cases can run into years and the overall cost may not be worth it so many try to settle, or involve bailiffs to recover assets.

WOMEN IN BUSINESS

Women dominate the Jamaican business landscape, though a glass ceiling still exists between them and the top jobs. Women today are often the main breadwinners, and within the office are treated and respected equally with the men.

chapter nine

COMMUNICATING

LANGUAGE

Many Jamaicans are bilingual—they speak Standard English and chat in patois, a form of Creole that fuses Spanish, African languages including Twee and Ibo, Amerindian, and English elements. Unless you've been exposed to patois it takes some time for your ear to get used to the words and phrases. Following the thread of conversations can be tricky, and that, combined with the speed with which Jamaicans interact with each other, can make it difficult to join in socially. There are a number of tourist dictionaries and other more scholarly works available that provide a literary insight into patois, but the reality is that the more exposure you have to it the more attuned your ear will become.

Many people feel it is rude to try to speak patois. It's a fine line, but it depends who you're speaking to. It's up to you to judge the situation. Most Jamaicans try to speak "properly" to foreigners, in an accent not surprisingly sounding like North American English, influenced as it has been by American movies and the large number of

Jamaicans who have spent time in the USA. However, many others, especially in the more rural parts of the country, don't understand Standard English, and the traditional behavior of speaking more loudly and clearly won't improve the situation. In such a case, attempting a few words of patois may make a difference. There is a glossary of Jamaican English terms on page 162.

Written Communication
There's a predilection in Jamaica for using grandiose words in writing that should really be left in the thesaurus. You often see this in academic work, but also in the newspapers—and, by extension, you hear it on the radio, too. Among the older generation this is quite common. The letters section in the newspapers gives away much about the evolution of English on the island. The broadsheet newspaper is *The Gleaner*.

FORMS OF ADDRESS
These depend on who you are talking to and the social circumstances. Lots of people will walk into a crowded waiting room or climb into the back of a packed route taxi and greet people with a courteous "Good morning," or whatever the time of day is. When people gather together socially you'll often hear women over fifty years old being addressed as "Mummy," and older men being called "Dads," or "Elder." In a more formal situation "Sir" and "Mr." are appropriate marks of respect, and you may

sometimes hear the more old-fashioned use of
"Miss" or "Mas" (short for Master) with the first
name, when the speaker is more established with a
family: "Miss Olive," or "Mas Gussie." Another
common form of address to followers of Rastafari is
"Ras," for example, "Ras Kwame."

GREETINGS

Jamaicans have so many greetings that seem
constantly to evolve and change. However, in
professional settings the handshake is the standard
greeting between men and women. In social
situations, especially between men, you'll notice a
wide range of handshakes or signs. The "terrorist
fist bump," as it is now termed in the USA, has been
in use for decades: each closing one hand into a fist,
they lightly tap the front of the fists together. The
handshake with thumbs exposed and the thumbs
then clicked three or more times was originally
done between Rastafari, but young men have now
taken this up, especially as a greeting.

DIRECTNESS AND EXPLETIVES

Jamaicans don't hide their feelings, and their
directness is often misinterpreted as aggression. The
banter is often loud, boisterous, and very physical.
An outsider may observe some conversations that
look and sound as if war is about to break out—but
it's just the way Jamaicans are. If you are white,
don't be surprised if someone calls you "Whitey,"

and if you are from eastern Asia you may be addressed as "Mr. Chin." It's just the easiest or most obvious way of differentiating you from others—there's rarely any intention to insult. If you carry some weight you'll be described as fatty, fluffy, or stout, and if you're a thin woman the term will be "slimmers." Again, these are not insults but just a very upfront way of distinguishing people.

Local Jamaican expletives are thrown around a lot. Words such as "bumbo" and "rass," which are relatively harmless on their own, become the worst combination when put with the term "clot," which means cloth. So "bumbo clot" is essentially a wipe for the bottom; "blood clot" is a menstrual pad; "rass" is another word for the behind or ass. This sort of thing may seem fairly harmless in comparison to traditional Anglo-Saxon swearwords, but can be more incendiary. If you do come across such terms, don't use them, as they are as insulting as the "f-word" in other countries. As in other nations in the region, you'll get used to people hissing, saying "psst" to attract someone's attention. It is common, especially when trying to get the attention of a foreigner.

HUMOR

Jamaica is one of the funniest countries on earth. People find humor in nearly every situation, and it's seen as a good way to deal with some of the harsh realities of life. Faced with a surly exterior, crack a smile and you'll receive one! Jamaicans will laugh at jokes, and are gifted in wordplay— the wit on display is razor sharp. People are ready to laugh at others' misfortunes, also, but if you laugh at someone else's expense to their face, making them feel small, you will be considered very rude, as you'll be seen to be belittling them.

The satire and bawdiness of pantomime are hugely popular. The country's comics and writers provide social commentary to the masses on TV and on stage. One of the island's biggest stars is a comic actor, Keith "Shebada" Ramsey, who plays on being effeminate. He is hugely popular, despite the homophobic attitudes that exist in the country, and there is more to his performances than playing to stereotypes.

BODY LANGUAGE

You can right away pick out Jamaicans who've lived abroad—their speed as pedestrians gives them away immediately. In Jamaica people walk at a much slower pace. Some of the younger men have taken this laid-back walk to an extreme, with an exaggerated "skank, " or bounce, that has become popular in African Caribbean communities around the globe.

Jamaican women friends often walk along the street holding hands. Men are never seen close together—they keep a distance between them because of the possible sexual connotations of even throwing an arm round a friend's shoulder—

such behavior can be seen as "funny," and elicit quizzical looks.

Jamaican Wiseass

A man from the Jamaican countryside had lost his house and all his crops after a hurricane. He had nothing left but his donkey. After days of being miserable, and not being able to find a job, he took his donkey into the city and put up a sign that read, "Betting $10.00 that this donkey could answer any question you ask."

One man came up saying: "No way that ass could tell me how much numbers in a phone number?" The owner said, "Tell him, ass?" The donkey stomped on the ground seven times, so the man paid and walked away shocked.

The next man came up and said, "Tell me how much players make up a football side?" The donkey stomped the ground eleven times. The man paid up.

By now, the news had spread like wildfire and people from near and far gathered around to see this smart ass.

A woman came out of the crowd, walked up to the owner and said, "You is ah fraud and ah bet $100.00 he cyan tell me meh age." The donkey stepped back, let go a loud fart and stomped his foot two times. The woman fainted. After a fan and some smelling salts and water, she revived and pointed at the donkey and say, "Buh how him know ah was farty-two?"

THE MEDIA

The main sources of information for most Jamaicans are television and radio, with newspapers being passed around many people as one person will buy one and share it with friends and even passersby.

Television and Radio

Jamaica, like much of the Caribbean, has a wide variety of radio stations providing a combination of talk and music, much of it reggae. There are sixteen stations that share the airwaves of Jamaica: BBC World Service, Fame FM, Hot 102, Irie FM, KLAS FM, Kool FM, Love 101, Megajamz, Music 99, Power 106, Radio 2, RJR, Roots FM, Zip 106, Radio Mona, and TBC (The Breath of Change) FM.

CVM and TVJ (Television Jamaica) are the main free-to-air TV stations and provide local news and current affairs with a variety of lifestyle programming from cooking to talent shows. Love TV is religious programming that is available in the larger towns, but other Christian broadcasts, like Mercy Truth Ministries Television and CETv, are available on cable only. Other services are available on subscription via Flow, a countrywide cable operator, other smaller local operators, or via the Dish Network out of the USA. Other local stations include music and entertainment from Hype TV and RETV and sports from CVM Plus, TVJ Sports Network, and Sportsmax.

The country was rocked in the summer of 2010 when police officers were seen beating a murder suspect and then apparently shooting him dead when he was subdued. The footage was shown on TV, used as crucial evidence in the investigation, and highlighted human rights abuses within the Jamaica Constabulary Force.

The Press

The country has nine newspapers: *The Gleaner*, *The Star*, *The Observer*, and *Chat*, which are daily, and *The North Coast Times*, *The News*, *The Western Mirror*, and *Mandeville Weekly*, plus *The Sunday Herald*.

The defamation laws in Jamaica are quite harsh but in general the country has a fair and free press. *The Gleaner* and *The Observer* are the two most widely read papers. *The Gleaner*, started in 1834, is the Caribbean's oldest paper. *The Observer* was founded in 1993 and is owned by Gordon "Butch" Stewart, who runs the Sandals resort chain. The partisanship rife in the 1970s is no more; journalists are more fair-minded and evenhanded than in the past, but with only three quality titles, if you include *The Sunday Herald*, the country has little diversity.

SERVICES
Telephone

There are very few public phone booths on the island because the high numbers of cell phones has made them redundant. The island has one of the highest concentrations of cell phones in the world, with 116 percent, as opposed to 89 percent in the USA. Many people have two or more phones to avoid paying the costs of calling people on different networks, and the competition between the networks is fierce. The Irish company Digicel has the greatest number of users, followed by Lime (formerly Cable and Wireless) and Claro, part of Mexican telecoms giant America Movil. Jamaica has become one of the key markets for these companies in the region, with all three spending heavily to grab customers from each other.

The cell phone has had a transforming effect on Jamaica socially. Those on low incomes, especially in rural communities, had few means of communicating with the outside world before the cell phone, and now information and services can be accessed by nearly all.

Landline use has dropped. Many people no longer have landlines, and if they do they use American cheap-rate options such as Magic Jack to reduce costs. The cable operator Flow has brought in Triple Play options of broadband, cable, and phone to Kingston and Montego Bay, but the rest of the island is still waiting for the service. The landline service is operated by Lime and provides good-quality calls. However, if you are calling from a private home or business premises you'll need a password to enable you to connect to numbers outside the country.

Internet

The Internet has grown quickly in Jamaica. The service is provided in most towns in the country, and broadband is available anywhere there is a phone line. Elsewhere, especially in more rural areas, the Web can be accessed by the use of USB dongle modems on prepaid contracts. There are Web cafés across the island for locals and tourists. The International Monetary Fund estimates that more than half the population now uses the Web. The disturbances in Tivoli Gardens in May 2010 aw many Jamaicans both in and out of the diaspora going online to social networking to find out the latest. Even though many of these sites were putting out unconfirmed reports, they were seen as the best way of getting the news as it happened. Some of the established broadcasters were also broadcasting news off the Web sites from "citizen journalists."

Mail

The mail service in Jamaica is slow, and for businesses courier services are more reliable and faster. A "wish you were here" postcard will more than likely arrive a few weeks after your vacation has ended. Airmail to the USA and Canada takes between one and two weeks, to Europe two to three weeks, and to Australasia three to four weeks.

CONCLUSION

So, the island of Jamaica is full of contradictions. It is rich in fauna and flora—the wildlife is simply spectacular, especially for bird-watchers. But the

need for food has seen its waters overfished to the point of near collapse. The "hill and gully" ride around the island in a route taxi will take in majestic mountains down to beautiful bays and

beaches, white sand, and turquoise seas.

Jamaica is the third-biggest Anglophone nation in the Americas, after the USA and Canada, and despite its small size it continues to punch above its weight. In its heyday it was one of the jewels in the crown of the British Empire. It saw prosperity in the postwar years, but the instability of the 1970s has meant the country is struggling to bounce back. In the 1980s the close bond with the Reagan administration in the USA brought hope, but as the geopolitical importance of the island waned so did its economic fortunes—yet Jamaicans battled on.

Culturally, Jamaica is a powerhouse that has created the sound of mento, ska, and reggae—still popular around the world; its most famous voice, Bob Marley, was one of the most important musicians of the twentieth century. This small island is also home to the world's fastest man in the shape of Usain Bolt, whose impressive turn of speed is in part credited to the Jamaican yellow yam and also to the tough rural life he was brought up in, along with a dedication to be the best despite lacking the opportunities of the developed world.

Jamaicans have a fire that has been hard to douse. It was burning when their forefathers arrived on slave ships, barely alive after the middle passage, and it was still there when the maroons fought the British to a truce in a guerrilla war that saw the establishment of the Maroon Treaty granting them freedom, the first between former slaves and the colonial authorities.

The Jamaican people have a warmth that is unmatched anywhere. They are unafraid to talk to strangers, they'll laugh at nearly anything, they'll discuss and debate with a passion, and they'll give it to you straight. They love life and they fear God. And it's these and many other traits that leave them content. The country regularly ranks in the top five happiest nations on earth in the annual Happy Planet Index.

Life in Jamaica is far from easy. The country is massively in debt, and is struggling to get back to its precolonial heyday, but it is free to chart its own history. Every August the nation marks Independence and Emancipation Day, cultural events that stir the soul as this small island celebrates its past and looks forward to its future. As the Jamaicans say, "Wi likkle but wi talawa." The country may be small, but it's a gutsy place with feisty people.

APPENDIX: SOME JAMAICAN ENGLISH TERMS

Article	respected, valued
A-go to	I'm going to go
Abeng	a cow's horn, blown by maroons during the wars against the English as a warning, now used in celebration
Almshouse	To be treated badly
Arredi	already, as in "Mi ready areddi"
Axe	ask, as in "Axe mi di question"
Babylon	the police or establishment
Backways	backward
Badda	bother, as in to bother someone
Bad mine	carrying a grudge, bitterness
Bad mout	speaking about others behind their back
Bad wud	swearing
Bandulu	to try to con somebody
Bangarang	a disturbance, riotous behavior
Bap	the sudden loss of something, as in "Him alive one minute and bap him gone"— he died suddenly
Bare	plenty of, as in "Is bare man inna di club"— it's all men in there
Bat	any large butterfly or moth that flies at night
Batty	bottom, backside
Bawl	to cry, especially if you get "licks" (a slap) or if you are in a highly emotional state
Bex	annoyed or upset
Boss	used by workers as a sign of respect to those in authority
Bruk	something is broken, or a sexual act
Bulla	A small round cake that's eaten with cheese
Bwoy	a child, or a male friend regardless of age

Chaka-chaka	a messy, untidy place or person.
Check	to see. "Check you later"—see you later
Cho!	expression of annoyance
Cooyah	exclamation of shock
Cotch	to rest somewhere for a short while
Cris	something that looks good, as in "What a cris cyar"—what an attractive vehicle
Dat	that
Di or de	the
Dem	them
Dis	this
Diyah	here
Dung	down
Duppy	ghost
Dutchy	large, round-bottomed, metal pot
Dutty	dirty
Dweet	do it, or did it
Elder	older people
Facety	cheeky
Fire	greeting to a Rasta man
Flim	film
Foreign	abroad, as in "Him gone a foreign"—he's gone to a foreign country
Galong	to go along
Ganja	the Hindi word for marijuana, a plant introduced to the island by indentured workers from India
Ginnal	a cheater, con artist, untrustworthy
Im	a useful word that can mean he, she, it, him, her, or there
Irie	okay or good
Ital	pure natural foods without salt

Jah	the name of God for Rastafari, from the Jewish Old Testament word for Jehovah
Jelly	a young coconut that has soft flesh and water inside
Jook	to poke with a finger or pierce with a stick or pin
Kiss me neck!	expression of shock and surprise
Kyan	can
Kyann	can't
Licky Licky	sucking up, fawning
Lilly bit	small, often in reference to children
Mauger, maga	meager, thin and slender
Marina	a man's vest, generally of the string type
Nyam	to eat
Pickney	child or infant
Poppy-show	this is used when someone is looking foolish or making others look bad (from puppet show)
Ras	from the Amharic title meaning lord, used by Rastafari
Rass	bottom, backside
Renk	something that smells bad
Screw	to look angry or upset
Sipple	slippery
Scliff	spliff, ganja joint
Talawa	something that is good
Tan	to stand, as in "Tan deh"—stand or wait there
Uno	you all
Wha gwan?	"What's going on?" used as a common greeting or a question about well-being
Zion	Ethiopia, or the promised land for Rastas

Further Reading

Bond, James. *Field Guide to Birds of the West Indies*. Boston, Mass.: Houghton Mifflin, 1979.

Bennett-Coverly, Louise. *Anancy and Miss Lou*. Kingston, Jamaica: Sangster's Book Stores, 1979.

Cassidy, Frederic Gomes, and Robert Brock Le Page. *Dictionary of Jamaican English*. Kingston, Jamaica: University of the West Indies Press, 2002.

Cezair-Thompson, Margaret. *The Pirate's Daughter*. New York: Random House, 2008.

Channer, Colin (ed). *Iron Balloons*. New York: Akashic Books, 2006.

Chevannes, Barry. *Rastafari: Roots and Ideology*. Syracuse, NY: Syracuse University Press, 1994.

McKay, Claude. *Banana Bottom*. London: Serpent's Tail, 2005.

Patterson, Orlando. *The Children of Sisyphus*. Harlow, Essex: Longman, 1982.

Senior, Olive. *The A-Z of Jamaican Heritage*. Kingston, Jamaica: Heinemann and Gleaner Company, 1984.

Thompson, Ian. *The Dead Yard: Tales of Modern Jamaica*. London: Faber and Faber 2009.

Winkler, Anthony C. *The Lunatic*. New York: Akashic Books, 2007.

culture smart! jamaica

Index

African religions 54–56
alcohol 95–97
Amerindian people 17
Anancy 107–8
Anglicans 33, 53–54
art 105–6
athletics 8, 103
attitudes toward others 35–36

Baptists 10, 33, 54, 110
Barbados 20, 21, 40, 138
"barrel children" 35, 73
bars 95, 99
bauxite/alumina 13, 31, 138
Beach Jovert 65
beaches 92, 97–98
beer 97
begging 74, 100
Belisario, Isaac Mendes 105, 120
Bennett, Louise 108
Bermuda (Somer islands) 20
birth 80
black Jamaicans 10, 15–16, 28
Black Nationalism 57
Black River, St. Elizabeth 14, 121
Blackwell, Chris 112, 119
Blue and John Crow Mountains Marine Park 13
Blue Lagoon 116
Blue Mountains 12, 14, 117
body language 154–55
Bogle, Paul 24, 25
Bolt, Usain 132, 160–61
Boscobel 65
Boston Bay, Portland 94
bribery 128
Britain, migration to 47–48, 49
British rule 9, 19–24, 47, 52, 160
bureaucracy 43, 69
Burning Spear 113

business relationship 144–45
Bustamante, Alexander 28
Buster, Prince 111

calypso 65, 110
capital flight 29
Carnival 36, 65
Catholic Church, Catholics 33, 52–53
character 8, 9, 35–36, 161
children 37
  attitudes toward 38
  growing up in Jamaica 84–89
Chinese 16, 52–53
Christians, Christianity 10, 32–34, 35, 52–54
Christmas Eve/Day 63
Chung, Brian "Ribbie" 109
Church of God 10, 54
cinema 113–14
climate 10, 14–15
clubs 77, 109
"coasters" 124–26
Cockpit Country, Trelawney 12, 14, 132
Cold War 9, 46
color, attitudes toward 50
Columbus, Christopher 17–18
Columbus, Diego 18
Congos, The 113
"cook shops" 92
cool Jamaica 46
corporal punishment 38
corruption 128, 129, 140, 145–46
Costa Rica 48, 140
Creoles 26
cricket 104
crime 29, 31, 47, 83, 91, 136–37, 140, 146
Cromwell, Oliver 19
cultural life 104–8
Culture Yard, Kingston 119
currency 11, 28–29

cycling 102, 130

daily life 81–84
dance 36, 77, 106–7, 108–9
dancehall 8, 45, 65, 107–10, 112
debt 31, 40, 143, 161
Dekker, Desmond 105, 111
Devon House 120
diaspora 35, 39, 49, 57, 60, 114, 159
directness 152–53
disagreement, managing 149
Dodd, Clement "Coxsone" 111
Dolphin Head Mountains 14
Dominican Republic 138
dons (local gangsters) 47, 136, 146
dress
  business 147
  invitations home 75–76
  Jamaican fashion sense 98
  school uniform 85, 87
drinking 95–97, 148
driving 126–29
drugs 47, 59–60, 136
Dunns River Falls 114–15

Easter Monday 61–62
eating out and eating in 92–94
economy 29, 30–31, 138–40
education 37, 43–44, 81–82, 85–88
elders, care of 35, 72
Elizabeth II, Queen 11
  attitude toward 47–48
Emancipation Day 62
employment 83
English Patois 10, 150, 151
Esquivel, Don Juan 18
ethnic makeup 10
exercise 101–2

expletives 153
extortion 47, 146
Eyre, Edward John 24,
25

Falmouth 118–19
family 34–35, 78–91
family occasions
79–81
first names 147
food 82, 94
foreigners, attitudes
toward 38–39
forms of address
151–52
Frenchman's Cove
116–17
friendliness 69–70
funerals 63, 81

ganja 59–60
Garvey, Marcus 57
George V, King 58
gift giving 72–74, 75,
146
Golding, Bruce 30
Good Friday 61
Gordon, George
William 25
government 11, 26
and business 142–44
government agencies
42
governor general (GG)
11, 27
Green Grotto Caves
116
greetings 71–72, 152
Grounations 59

Haile Selassie,
Emperor of Ethiopia
57, 58, 59
Hall, Governor-
General Kenneth 30
handshake 71–72
health 132–36
health services 89–90
Hellshire Beach 92
Hellshire Hills 14
Heritage, Morgan 60
Hibbert, Toots 111
"higglers" 83
Hispaniola 12, 19
history 16–26
origins and conquest
17–18
the English
occupation 19–21

the plantation
economy 21–22
the Maroon Wars
22–23
the abolition of
slavery 23–24
rebellion 24–26
HIV 135–36
Ho Lung, Father
Richard 53
home ownership 45
homosexuality 51, 76
hotels 15, 93–94, 131,
133

housing 90–91
Howell, Leonard 58
humor 35, 147, 153–54
hurricanes 10, 13,
14–15

independence 9, 17,
26, 46, 47
Independence Day 62
insects 134–35
International
Monetary Fund
(IMF) 29, 30, 159
Internet 11, 159
invitations home
75–76
Isaacs, Gregory 113
"Ital" food 60, 93

Jamaica Georgian
Society 71
Jamaica Labour Party
(JLP) 27, 28, 30, 46,
85–86, 90, 136
Jamaican businesses
140–41
Jamaican English
terms 162–64
Jamaican traditions
63–64
Jehovah's Witnesses 54
jerk cooking 94
Johnkanoo 64

Kapo 121
Kingston 8, 10, 14,
46–47, 49, 53, 65,
71, 84, 90, 94, 98,
109, 113, 120, 121,
132, 133, 136, 139,
146
kite festivals 61
Kumina 10, 55, 56

Labor Day 62, 72
laid-back attitude 41,
46
languages 10, 40,
150–51
Lee, Byron 65
Leeward Maroons 22
literacy 85
literature 107–8
Little Ochie 94

macho culture 50–51
Mandeville 10, 16, 84,
90
Mangroves 13
Manley, Edna 105–6,
121
Manley, Michael 28,
29, 113
Manley, Norman 27,
105
Marley, Bob 8, 110–13,
115, 160
Marley, Rita 115
maroons 20, 22–23,
161
mass migration 29
May Pen 10, 14, 90
meals 82–83
media 11, 156–57
meeting people 70–71
meetings, business
146–47
mento 110, 111, 112,
160
Middle Passage 21
migrants 16
migration 48–49
minibuses 82, 124–26
Missionaries of the
Poor 53
mixed heritage
Jamaicans 10, 16
money, attitudes
toward 49–50
Montego Bay 10, 16,
65, 71, 77, 84, 90,
109, 113, 132, 133,
136, 146
Montego Bay Marine
Park 13, 118
Moravians 54
Moray Bay Rebellion
(1866) 24–26
Motta, Stanley 111
multiculturalism 20
murder 36, 47, 140
music 8, 45, 46, 65, 97,
101, 109–13, 156,

160
Naipaul, V.S. 108
National Heroes Day
  63
national holidays 61
negotiations 148–49
Negril 10, 13, 39, 71,
  77, 109, 121, 132
Negril Marine Park 13
newspapers 11, 151,
  157
nightlife 108–14
Nine Miles 115
Nine Nights 64
Nyabingis 59

Obeah 56
Ocho Rios 10, 77, 90,
  109, 113, 132
omens, good and bad
  luck 66–67
other islanders 39–41

Patterson, P. J. 30
patty shops 93
Pentecostals 10, 33, 110
People's National Party
  (PNP) 27, 28, 30, 46,
  136, 142–43
Perry, Lee "Scratch"
  113
pharmacies 133
photography 75
Pinnacle 58
places to visit 114–21
plantocracy 26
Pocomania (Poco)
  55–56
police 128, 129, 136,
  137, 157
political attitudes
  46–47
politics 26–30
population 10, 15–16
Port Antonio 10, 14,
  117
Port of Spain, Trinidad
  40
Port Royal 20–21, 121
Portland 132
Portmore 10, 136
presentations 147
press, the 157
pride 32, 70, 71
prostitution 47, 77

R&B 111
Ramsey, Keith
  "Shebada" 154

Rastafari 10, 56–61,
  110, 112, 113, 152
reggae 8, 59, 65, 108,
  109, 110, 112–13,
  156, 160
Reid, Duke 111
religion 10, 32–34,
  52–61, 63
restaurants 94, 98, 148
returnees 16
Revivalism 10
rich/poor divide 16, 49
Rio Grande 117
road travel 122–23
"robots" 124
rocksteady 112
Rose Hall 117–18
route taxis 123–24
"rude boys" 112
rum 96
  shacks 95, 99

safety 136–37
St. Andrew 136
St. Jago de la Vega 18
San Antonio 132
Santiago 17, 18
Seaga, Edward 30, 113
Second World War
  48–49
sense of style 44–45
service industries 41
Seventh-day Adventist
  10, 33, 54
sexual encounters
  36–37
shopping malls, town
  squares and 100–101
Simpson-Miller, Portia
  30
ska 8, 110, 111–12,
  160
slavery 18, 20–24, 41,
  53, 55, 161
Small, Millie 112
soca 65, 110
soccer 104
socialism 9, 28, 46
socializing with the
  opposite sex 76–77
Spanish rule 18, 20, 52,
  116
Spanish Town 10, 136
sports 102–4
stomach upsets 133
sugar industry 21–22
sunburn 134

Tainos (Arawaks)

17–20, 105
taxation 144
taxis 82, 99, 100–101,
  123–24
telephone 11, 158–59
television 11, 83,
  156–57
tennis 102
theater 113, 114
timekeeping 72, 147
tipping 99
Toots and the Maytals
  105
Tosh, Peter 113
tourism 31, 38, 93–94,
  100, 136–37, 138
town squares and
  shopping malls
  100–101
trade 20, 139–40
trade unions 27, 142
Trinidad and Tobago
  40, 65, 138

unemployment 83, 142
United States,
  migration to 48, 49
Universal Negro
  Improvement
  Association 57
universal suffrage 26,
  27–28
University of the West
  Indies 41

vaccinations 133
vegetarianism 60–61,
  93
violence 8, 29, 40–41,
  46

Wailer, Bunny 113
Walcott, Derek 108
water, drinking 133–34
weddings 63, 80–81
white Jamaicans 16
wildlife 160
Windward Maroons 22
women
  attitudes towards 37
  in business 149
  gender role
    stereotypes 79
work 41–43
workforce 141–42
World Bank 140
written communication
  151